lonely planet

POCKET GENOA & CINQUE TERRE

Brendan Sainsbury

Top: Genoa's *caruggi* (p44)
Bottom: Portofino (p53)

Contents

Plan Your Trip 4

POCKET GENOA & CINQUE TERRE

Explore Genoa & Cinque Terre 31

Genoa & Cinque Terre Toolkit 143

FROM TOP LEFT: CAVAN-IMAGES/SHUTTERSTOCK ©, SURATWADEE RATTANAJARUPAK/SHUTTERSTOCK ©

★ Top Experiences

The Journey Begins Here

Genoa and Cinque Terre are part of a mountainous coastal strip in northwest Italy that lies entirely within the region of Liguria. Despite challenging topography, the area is heavily populated with elegant beach resorts and handsomely dishevelled fishing villages that often defy the rugged terrain. Hillside walking paths connect ancient sanctuaries, houses stack up behind diminutive ports, and tiny pebble and sand beaches inhabit sheltered coves. Welcome to a land of maze-like alleyways and palm-lined promenades crowned by luxuriant palaces and dusted with the crusty heritage of one of Europe's finest maritime cities.

Brendan Sainsbury

@sainsburyb

Brendan has written over 70 Lonely Planet guidebooks and covered 17 of Italy's 20 regions. This was his fourth time researching the Italian Riviera.

Vernazza (p89)

THE BEST

Art Experiences

Genoa has a huge art heritage, much of it packed inside its opulent Palazzi Rolli with plenty more colour etched onto the walls of its baroque churches. Masterful artworks lie further along the Riviera too.

Evaluate the subtleties of Genoa's baroque-era masters, including Bernardo Strozzi, in the lavish confines of the **Palazzo Rosso**. (p39)

Take your Italian art education into the 19th and 20th centuries at the **Galleria d'Arte Moderna** in the Genoa suburb of Nervi. (p47)

See works by Flemish painter Peter Paul Rubens in the intricately frescoed **Chiesa del Gesù**. (pictured; p45)

See the haunting *Crucifixion* that may (or may not) have been painted by Van Dyck in Monterosso's **Convento dei Cappuccini**. (p77)

Unwrap La Spezia's surprising stash of Renaissance art, including Old Masters Titian and Tintoretto, in the city's **Museo Amedeo Lia**. (p129)

See Genoa's only known Caravaggio, *Ecce Homo*, in the noble **Palazzo Bianco**. (pictured; p38)

Right: *Ecce Homo*, Palazzo Bianco

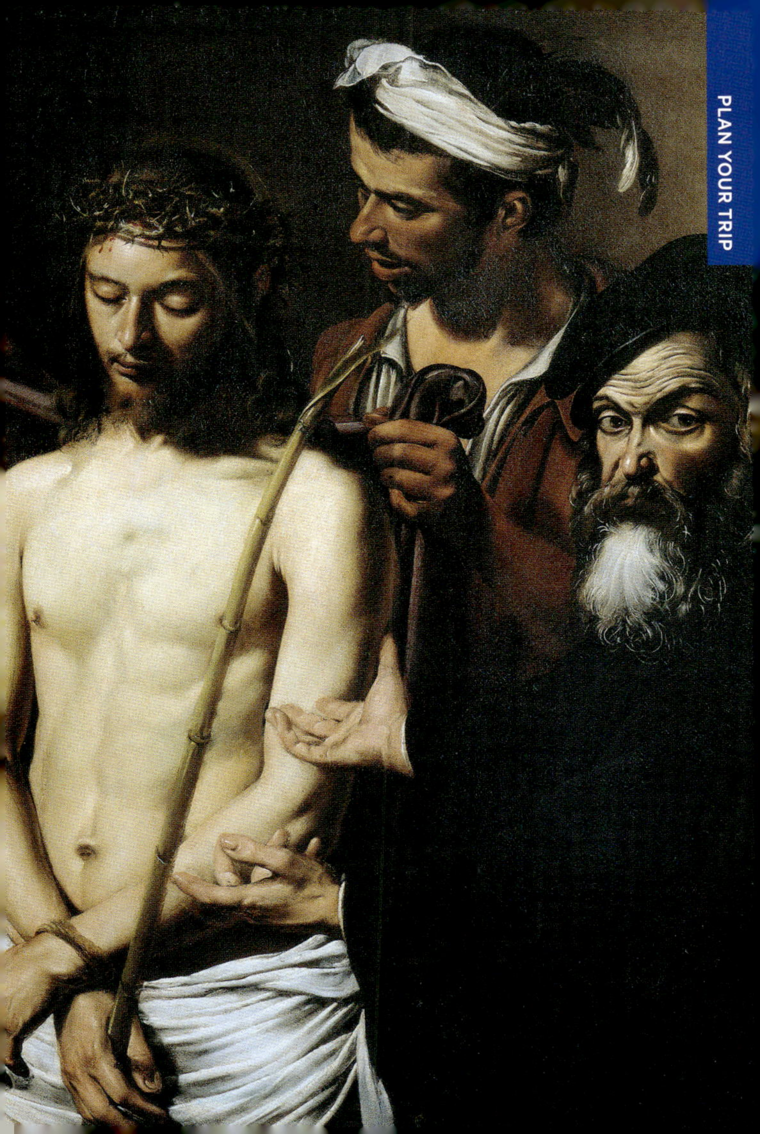

THE BEST

Water Experiences

Liguria is a thin coastal region where nowhere is far from the sea. So why ignore it? Water-based activities range from swimming and paddling to taxiing around on boats as a means of getting from A to B.

Hire a board and wetsuit (or bring your own) and hit the beach in Levanto for some of Italy's most explosive **surf breaks**. (p64)

Discover a tranquil way to see all five Cinque Terre villages in one day by taking to the seas and **kayaking** out of Riomaggiore. (p123)

Jump from a rock or paddle out from the beach and embrace some of Liguria's clearest water in **San Fruttuoso**. (pictured; p56)

Dip beneath the waves in a protected marine park in the waters off Cinque Terre with seasoned diving operators, **Diving 5 Terre**. (p124)

Go in search of whales, dolphins and other marine wildlife on an organised whale-watching trip out of Genoa with **Consorzio Liguria Via Mare**. (pictured; p47)

Cinque Terre vineyards

THE BEST

Gastronomic Experiences

In the unofficial poll to find the world's best food, Italy invariably wins by a landslide. The key is in the simplicity, a field in which Genoa excels with restaurants that concoct fabulous pesto, focaccia, anchovies and *farinata* (chickpea flour flat bread).

Stop for lunch in a no-nonsense, old **Genoa trattoria** and enjoy an experience that hasn't changed much since Columbus. (p48)

Try your luck with a pestle and mortar and attempt to grind pesto the Vernazza way in a cooking class with **Cinque Sensi**. (p95)

Join a giant fish fry-up on the harbourside at Camogli's **Sagra del Pesce** festival in May. (p63)

Pause mid-hike in the terraced vineyards of **Cantina Capellini** above Cinque Terre where you can sip local DOCs with a plate of *bruschette* and absorb one of Italy's finest views. (p117)

Gravitate to **Monterosso al Mare**, the region's anchovy capital, to sample the small salty fish with a glass of local wine at a streetside *enoteca* (wine bar). (p81)

THE BEST

Hiking Experiences

Hiking is one of the understated joys of Italy, and Liguria – most notably Cinque Terre – guards a honeycomb of coastal trails, many of them heavily imbued with history.

Hike in a broad curve around the rocky coastline of the **Portofino peninsula** starting in Camogli and finishing in Santa Margherita Ligure. (pictured; p58)

Inhale pine, wine and the sea air while traversing steeply terraced vineyards on the **Manarola–Corniglia trail**. (p106)

Follow in the footsteps of erstwhile penitents and pilgrims on the steep path to Rapallo's **Santuario Basilica di Montallegro**. (p55)

Take the long, refreshingly uncrowded **Alta Via delle Cinque Terre** along the forested ridges between Porto Venere and Levanto. (pictured; p70)

Fall into step on Cinque Terre's walking 'highway', the **Sentiero Verde-Azzurro**, a historic rollercoaster that crosses terraced hillsides chock-a-block with astounding scenery. (p84)

Right: Vernazza, from the Sentiero Verde-Azzurro

THE BEST

Beach Experiences

Anywhere that has sea access, a hint of warm sun and enough space to lay down a towel can qualify as a beach in Italy. Not surprisingly, coastal Liguria is home to some of the nation's finest.

Clean out your wallet and sunbathe 'business class' at a deluxe beach club on tiny **Spiaggia di Paraggi** near Portofino. (pictured; p60)

Bring a surfboard, pull up a bicycle or just be a spectator on the action-packed beach strip in **Levanto**. (p64)

Feel the full force of the incoming waves on the ruggedly romantic shores of **Spiaggia di Fossola** in Riomaggiore. (p124)

Walk the promenade at **Spiaggia di Fegina** in Monterosso al Mare, Cinque Terre's only genuinely sandy beach with an array of private beach clubs to choose from. (p81)

Sunbathe within sight of two commanding forts on the once disputed (but now peaceful) beach zone of **San Terenzo** on the Bay of Poets. (pictured; p134)

THE BEST

Museum Experiences

Italy is home to some of the world's museum heavyweights and Genoa has its fair share. Its finest treasures can be found in the majestic Palazzi Rolli but there are other less celebrated collections in the region's outlying towns.

Eyeball art, furniture, architecture, gardens and vintage violins in Genoa's finest museum experience with exhibits spread over three separate palaces in the **Musei di Strada Nuova**. (p38)

Find an excuse to visit seaside Sestri Levante by calling into the **Museo Archeologico e della Città** to see some of Liguria's oldest finds. (p64)

Admire the detailed collection of seafaring exhibits put together by the Italian navy in the **Museo Tecnico Navale**. (p134)

Take a metaphoric voyage from Columbus to modern cruise liners in the **Galata Museo del Mare**, widely considered to be one of the best maritime museums in Europe. (p46)

Investigate the eclectic and sometimes eccentric collection of cultural artifacts amassed by world traveller Enrico Alberto d'Albertis in Genoa's **Castello d'Albertis**. (p43)

Castello d'Albertis

MATE KAROLY/SHUTTERSTOCK ©

Santa Margherita Ligure

THE BEST

Cafe Experiences

Having long resisted the adoption of international coffee franchises, Italian cafes exist in a category of their own. Some are as old as the Risorgimento. Many have harboured famous guests.

Reflect on life, cakes and good coffee in the mirrored confines of Genoa's vintage **Caffè degli Specchi**. (p50)

Savour some caffeine in Rapallo's **Cafe Pasticceria Canepa 1862**, serving coffee since before cappuccinos were invented. (p68)

Park yourself on an outdoor bench at Corniglia's **À Cáneva** and re-bolster your energy with a strong Lavazza. (p105)

Swerve past the glitzy hotels and haughty villas of Santa Margherita Ligure and opt instead for coffee and croissants at **Pasticceria Oneto**. (p68)

Relax after a day of hiking with a coffee and a slice of cake in **Cappun Magru** in Manarola's intimate Piazzale Papa Innocenzo IV. (p116)

Best for Kids

Step into Europe's second largest **aquarium** in Genoa for an entertaining and educational foray into the lives and times of the sea creatures of the Mediterranean. (p35)

Hire bicycles in Levanto and take a flat **seaside bike path** through old railway tunnels to the villages of Bonassola and Framura. (p66)

Take the train or funicular up to Genoa's **Ring of Forts** and discover a giant open-air playground on the cusp of the region's largest city. (p40)

Stake your claim for an umbrella and sun lounger in a private beach club in **Levanto** where the sand is soft and the water is patrolled by lifeguards. (p64)

Travel high above the hillside foliage to a glittering renaissance sanctuary on Rapallo's vintage **cable car**. (p55)

Best for Free

Avoid trail fees and spend a day or two walking along the ridgetops of Cinque Terre's **AV5T Trail**. (p70)

Hone your navigational skills in Genoa's **caruggi** (narrow streets) absorbing the sights and sounds of the maze-like city centre. (p44)

Hike into **San Fruttuoso**, lay down your towel on a free slice of beach and enjoy swimming in the crystalline bay. (p57)

Unravel mystery, history and priceless art by dipping into Genoa's **Cattedrale di San Lorenzo** to learn about frescoes and World War II bombs. (p45)

Join the masses on the region's finest early-evening stroll, dodging the crowds on the **Passeggiata Anita Garibaldi** in the Genovese suburb of Nervi. (p47)

Perfect Days

With the urban grit of Genoa complemented by the harmonious villages of Cinque Terre and plenty of chic Riviera resorts in between, a minimum of three days is best.

Palazzo Reale (p42)

FROM LEFT: TRABANTOS/SHUTTERSTOCK ©, MAUDANROS/SHUTTERSTOCK ©, SANTI RODRIGUEZ/SHUTTERSTOCK ©, SIMON DANNHAUER/SHUTTERSTOCK ©

DAY ONE

Only Have One Day?

MORNING

Nurse a breakfast cappuccino in **Caffe degli Specchi** (p50) before attempting to decipher the complex cartography of Genoa's *caruggi* (narrow streets) on your way down to Porto Antico. Choose one portside attraction over which to linger until lunchtime: **Galata Museo del Mare** (p46) for grown-ups, **aquarium** (p35) for kids.

AFTERNOON

After a *panino* in **Cairoli Cafe** (p51), dedicate the afternoon to the exquisite gardens and rich baroque finery of **Palazzo Reale** (p42). If you have time, press on to the **Palazzo Spinola** (p44; available on a joint ticket)

EVENING

Join the dinner queue outside **Trattoria delle Grazie** (pictured; p48) and finish the night sipping wine and admiring frescoes in boho **Les Rouges** (p50).

DAY TWO

A Weekend Trip

MORNING

Get an early train to **Monterosso al Mare** (p73). Walk along **Spiaggia di Fegina** (p81) and take a peep inside the **Convento dei Cappuccini** (p77) before hiking the **Sentiero Verde-Azzurro** (SVA) to Vernazza (p84).

AFTERNOON

Head down to Vernazza's **harbour** (pictured; p93) for lunch. Check out the waterside church and browse the shops in Via Roma. Grab an ice cream in **Il Porticciolo** (p96) before continuing along the SVA towards Corniglia.

EVENING

Stop in **Il Gabbiano** (p85) in Prevo on the SVA for an aperitif before arriving in Corniglia in time for dinner at **Ristorante Cecio** (p105). Admire the view from **Belvedere di Santa Maria** (p104) before catching a train back to Genoa.

DAY THREE

A Short Break

MORNING

Take the train to Riomaggiore and go for a slow amble around the village pausing at the **church** and the **oratory** (p124) before descending to the marina. Sign up for a two-hour **kayak tour** (p123) and get a chance to see the caves, cliffs and inlets that punctuate the Cinque Terre coast.

AFTERNOON

After lunch in **Via Colombo** (p121), hike the steep **Via Beccara** (p114) to Manarola (pictured). Rest your legs surveying the local action in **Piazzale Papa Innocenzo IV** (p113) before browsing the shops in **Via Discovolo** (p111) and gravitating back to the sea.

EVENING

As the light fades, head for snacks and sundowners at **Nessun Dorma** (p113), a spectacular bar whose sea-facing terrace sits atop the menacing rocks of **Punta Bonfiglio** (p114).

If You Have More Time

Get to know the charismatic neighbourhoods and parks on the cusp of Genoa, including the **Parco delle Mura** (p40) with its ring of semi-ruined forts, the erstwhile fishing village of **Boccadasse** (p47), and the museums and promenades of suburban **Nervi** (p47).

The three main villages on the eastern side of the Golfo dei Poeti deserve at least a day trip. **San Terenzo** (p134) is known for its sandy beach, **Lerici** (p136) has a tall, imposing **castle** (p136) and **Tellaro** (p138) sports a waterside church, site of a peculiar octopus legend. Pretty trails and promenades link all three.

Another potential day trip is **Porto Venere** (p130), famed for its sea-eroded Grotta di Byron and accessible through the illustrious naval port of La Spezia, home to a superb **naval museum** (p134).

Boccadasse (p47)

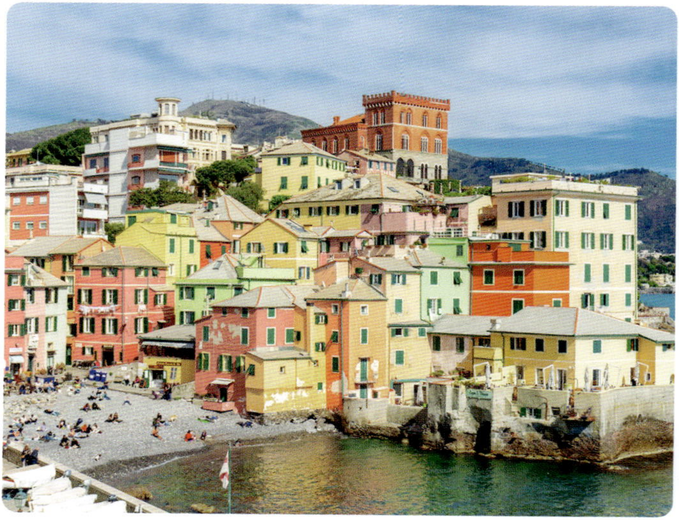

A City Day Trip

Take a train to Santa Margherita Ligure (pictured) before walking down to the harbour and hopping on a boat to **San Fruttuoso** (p56). Enjoy a dip in the sea, make a visit to the **abbey** (p56) and savour a seafood lunch at **La Cantina** (p67).

As the heat dissipates, hike 4km along the clifftops to **Portofino** (p60) and allow yourself at least one overpriced *aperitif* in the poseur-filled **Piazzetta** (p60).

If you have enough time and energy, head briskly up to **Castello Brown** (p60) for gorgeous views and mercifully cheap coffee. Return to Santa Margherita by bus and stop for dinner in a waterfront pizzeria.

On a Rainy Day

Stay dry in the morning by assessing breakfast options underneath the porches of Genoa's **Porto Antico** (pictured; p34) before making a dash across the esplanade for the **aquarium** (p35), where only the marine life gets wet.

Then, head north through the *caruggi* to Genoa's intriguing **cathedral** (p45) and affiliated **Museo del Tesoro** (p46), and spend the rest of the afternoon forgetting the foul weather in the maze of interconnecting rooms that make up the **Musei di Strada Nuova** (p38).

When evening arrives, follow the grand porches of Via Settembre XX to the covered **Mercato Orientale** (p49) where you'll find multiple dining options clustered under the same roof.

Get Prepared

BOOK AHEAD

Three months before
Book accommodation, particularly if visiting during the high season (June through early September). Ensure your passport is up to date.

One week before
Book tables at top restaurants. Reach out to tour operators like **Arbaspàa** (p115) and reserve outdoor activities, vineyard tours and other excursions.

A few days before
Check the weather forecast on the Riviera and prepare accordingly. Add apps like Google Translate and Trenitalia (Italy's rail network) to your phone.

Manners Matter

- Italy is a surprisingly formal society. Greet people in shops, restaurants and bars with a *'buongiorno'* (good morning) or *'buonasera'* (good evening); kiss both cheeks and say *'come stai'* (how are you) to friends.
- Cover your shoulders, torso and thighs and take off your baseball cap/hat when visiting churches.
- Italians are more inclined to dress relatively smartly when eating out.
- Queue-jumping is common in Italy: be polite but assertive.

Coffee Etiquette

Ligurians, like most Italians, drink small measures of coffee in regular amounts. If you want an espresso, just ask for a *caffè* (the word 'espresso' is rarely used in Italy). Cappuccinos are usually imbibed swiftly in the morning from small porcelain cups with a *brioche* (croissant) on the side. Don't bring your laptop, don't order a 20oz Americano, and don't expect a takeaway cup.

Things to Know

Always carry a little cash. Some restaurants and hotels only accept cash, while unattended petrol (gas) stations don't always accept foreign credit cards.

Pack some decent footwear if you're walking in Cinque Terre. Flip-flops/sandals don't cut it and aren't technically allowed on the SVA trail.

Italians tend to eat dinner later than Northern Europeans and Americans but not as late as Spaniards. Restaurants generally close between lunch and dinner. Most reopen around 7.30pm. Avoid restaurants with touts and a mediocre menu *turistico* (tourist menu).

Eat pasta with a fork, not a spoon. It's OK to eat pizza with your hands if bought *al taglio* (by the slice), but in restaurants it's more common (and Italian) to use a knife and fork.

TIPPING

Italians are not big tippers, and service is usually included in the restaurant bill. If you would like to tip, use cash. Italian credit card machines rarely have a tipping option.

Restaurants
No obligation, but 10% for good service

Bars & Cafes
Unusual to tip

Taxis
Round-up fare

Hotel staff
For good service

DAILY BUDGET

Budget: Less than €100

- Dorm bed: €20–35
- Double room in a budget hotel: €60–110
- Pizza or pasta: €6–15

Midrange: €100–250

- Double room in a hotel: €110–200
- Local restaurant dinner: €25–45
- Museum admission: €4–18

Top end: More than €250

- Double room in a four- or five-star hotel: €200 plus
- Top restaurant dinner: €45–150
- Opera ticket: €40–210

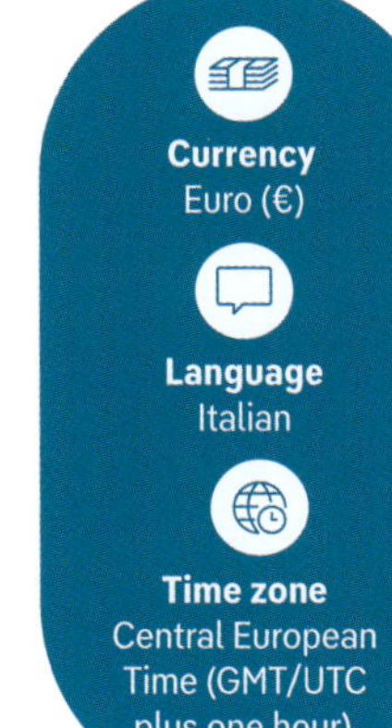

DISCOUNT CARDS

The two regional discount cards worth having are the **Genoa Museum Card**, valid in 28 city museums, and the **Cinque Terre Trekking Card**, which gives you access to the popular hiking trails.

ANTONIO TRUZZI/SHUTTERSTOCK ©

When To Go

The Italian Riviera has a mild climate with temperatures rarely dropping below freezing. To maximise outdoor activities, visit between April and October.

Summer rules in the Italian Riviera, with sun and tourists at annual highs. Crowds pack Cinque Terre from June to early September, a good time for beachgoing, hiking and other outdoor activities. March to May can be wet, though you can beat the crowds and score low-season discounts on lodging.

Late September and October can be an excellent time to visit, with pleasant weather and fewer tourists. Many hotels, restaurants and shops close in winter. Rainy weather can make hiking treacherous, and some walking trails close.

The Big Events

December/January For one of Cinque Terre's finest spectacles, you need to visit Manarola between early December and early January for its famous **Presepe** (p114), the largest floodlit nativity scene in the world.

June Sestri Levante (p63) hosts the **Andersen Premio Festival** (dedicated to the memory of Hans Christian Andersen).

July **Barcarolata** in Sestri Levante (p63) is a flotilla of boats decked out in extravagant papier-mâché decorations).

August La Spezia's famous **Palio del Golfo** (p133) rowing competition in August.

Food Festivals

Italy in general and Liguria in particular go mad for food festivals year-round. Some date back over a century. Fish and the celebration of the sea are obvious highlights.

Genoa Weather

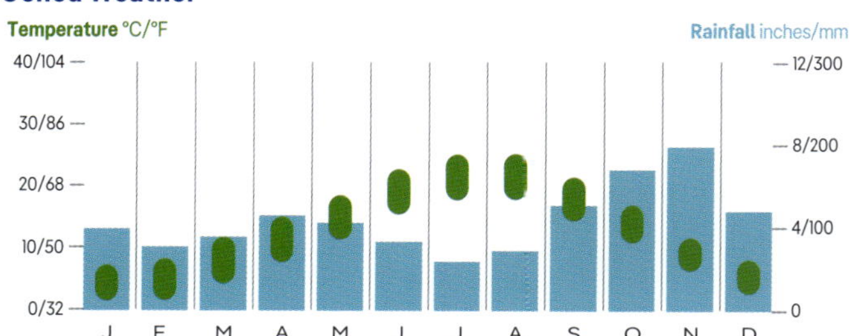

Palio del Golfo (p133)

May A lemon bonanza comes to Monterosso al Mare in May's **Sagra del Limone** (p82), when the town turns yellow, showcasing the zesty fruit in everything from cakes to ice cream.

May For a fish extravaganza, head to Camogli for the **Sagra del Pesce** (p63), where homage is paid to San Fortunato, the patron saint of fishers. A giant fish fry-up is held on the harbourside.

Early June Every odd-numbered year in early June, Genoa adopts the **Slow Fish** moniker (p151) with markets, tastings and workshops around Porto Antico.

September In addition to lemons, Monterosso is famed for anchovies, enthusiastically promoted in annual festivals. The closing of anchovy season is saluted in the **Sagra dell'Acciuga Salata** (p82) with salted fish laid out to sample.

November More culinary panache is displayed at Sestri Levante's **Sagra del Pane dell'Olio**, a showcase for Ligurian olive oil with workshops, cooking shows and guided tours.

ACCOMMODATION LOWDOWN

Accommodation rates can fluctuate enormously depending on the season, with Easter, summer and the Christmas/New Year period being the typical peak tourist times. It pays to book ahead in high season, especially in popular coastal areas in the summer when demand is extremely high.

Getting There

International travellers often enter the region through Genoa's Cristoforo Colombo Airport. However, it's also feasible to fly into Florence, Turin or even Nice, and catch a train.

From the Airport to the City Centre

By Bus & Train

AMT runs an Airlink shuttle from the airport to Stazione Genova Sestri Ponente-Aeroporto from where you can catch a train for the 15-minute journey into Piazza Principe. Shuttles run every 15 minutes or so.

By Bus

The AMT Volabus runs to/from Genoa's two main train stations (Piazza Principe and Brignole). Services are at least hourly between 5am and 11.45pm to the airport, and 5.50am to 12.20am from the airport. Buy tickets for the 30-minute journey on board *(€10)*. Credit cards accepted.

By Taxi

A taxi to or from the airport will cost around €20 to €30 depending on traffic. Genoa's airport is very centrally located. The journey time to Piazza Principe is only around 15 minutes.

Other Points of Entry

Genoa's Stazione Principe & Stazione Brignole

Genoa's two main railway stations are linked by very frequent trains to Milan (1½ to two hours), Pisa (two hours), Rome (five hours) and Turin (two hours).

Stazione Principe tends to have more trains, particularly going west to San Remo (two hours) and Ventimiglia (2½ hours).

La Spezia Centrale is another major regional hub with regular trains to Pisa, Florence and Rome.

Ferry Terminal

The terminal is in **Porto Antico** (Old Port) conveniently close to the historic centre. From here, ferries arrive and depart to Tangier (Morocco), Barcelona (Spain), Tunisia, Corsica (France), Sardinia and Sicily (Italy).

Getting Around

Liguria is a narrow region that hugs the coast, with nowhere more than 30km from the sea. It's easily accessible by public transport and trains are the primary modus operandi. Most sights between Genoa and Cinque Terre have mainline stations. Portofino and the Bay of Poets require short bus rides.

Train

The railway is the ultimate way to get around in Liguria with the entire coast connected by comfortable and economical trains. Regional services that stop at most stations are super frequent and rarely inordinately late. Most services are run by Trenitalia, Italy's state-run railway. The one exception is the Ferrovia Genova Casella, run as part of Genoa's local AMT system.

Bus

Buses connect La Spezia to the villages of the Bay of Poets (including San Terenzo, Lerici, Tellaro and Portovenere) all of which are off the train network. There are also useful bus services between Santa Margherita Ligure and Portofino, and Cinque Terre and some of its surrounding hamlets. The bus between Corniglia and its train station (avoiding the 377-step Lardarina) is particularly popular.

Car

With ample trains and boats stopping at even the smallest villages, there's little need for a car in Liguria. The A10 and A12 autostrade (motorways) run west–east across the entire region.

ESSENTIAL APP

The **Trenitalia App** enables quick check-in and real-time status updates for Italian trains.

FROM LEFT: PORNPRASIT PANADA/SHUTTERSTOCK ©, MIKADUN/SHUTTERSTOCK ©

Lifts & Funiculars

A series of lifts and funiculars connect Genoa's city centre with the hilly neighbourhoods to the north. The Ascensore Montegalletto near Piazza Principe station is a unique cabin that travels both horizontally and vertically, switching halfway between funicular and elevator to reach the Castello d'Albertis. The Spianata Castelletto elevators access the famous belvedere (lookout) on two sides: the eastern lift is encased in a sleek, glass art-nouveau tower, while the western one sports a plush wooden interior.

The Zecca–Righi funicular is a cable railway dating from the late 19th century that links the city centre with the Parco delle Mura in little over 15 minutes.

In Riomaggiore in Cinque Terre, a couple of lifts connect the train station with the upper parts of town. There are also lifts in La Spezia and Lerici.

Metro

Genoa has a single-line subway system that interconnects with the main Piazza Principe train station.

Boat

Various companies run passenger boats between cities and towns on the Riviera di Levante including La Spezia, Cinque Terre, Rapallo, Portofino, Camogli and Genoa. Some are seasonal, others run year-round. Beware: choppy seas can lead to last-minute cancellations.

Walking

Genoa is highly walkable, especially if you stick to the mostly pedestrianised *caruggi* (narrow streets) and the old port. The Cinque Terre villages are car-free and connected by well-signposted footpaths.

Public Transport Essentials

Train Reservations

Most of the train travel within the Genoa–Cinque Terre region is on regional trains. Reservations are not required. Seat reservations are necessary on Intercity (IC) and AV trains (the Frecciarossas).

Luggage

There is no big issue with luggage, and no luggage charges or baggage cars on Italian trains. Bring whatever you can carry and store it on board.

Passes

A MetDaily pass costs €10 and is valid for 24 hours on all Genoa's public transport plus the Genova–Casella railway, airport bus and bus 782 to Portofino.

The Cinque Terre Treno MS Card includes unlimited train and bus travel between Levanto and La Spezia (incorporating all five Cinque Terre villages). You can choose between one-, two- or three-day options. Prices fluctuate depending on the season.

PORTOFINO BUS

The bus from Portofino to Santa Margherita Ligure is crowded and expensive (€5). It's far more pleasant to walk (4km).

TRAVEL COSTS

Urban bus tickets
€2

Cinque Terre Treno MS Card (one-/two-/three-day passes)
from €19.50/34/46.50

Regional train from Genoa to La Spezia
from €9.70

TICKETS

- Multilingual ticket machines (called *biglietto veloce*) exist at all Italian train stations and are easy to use. They accept both cash and credit cards. Large stations also have ticket clerks during office hours.
- Regional train tickets that aren't dated must be time-stamped in green and grey *convalida* machines located in the stations before boarding the train.
- Single-fare tickets for any of Genoa's public transport options (bus, lifts, funicular and metro) cost €2. You can buy tickets in tabacchi, bars, small shops, tourist information offices or with the AMT Genova mobile app. Validate tickets on the bus/train. When validated, they remain valid for 110 minutes.

A Few Surprises

It's not all about gelato flavours and posing in the piazza. Here's how to see the Riviera beyond the obvious tourist haunts.

World War II Defences

Most of the fighting in World War II went on in southern and central Italy. Nonetheless, Liguria, strategically located on the coast, installed a muscular arc of military emplacements designed to ward off potential Allied attacks. Look out for concrete pillboxes, like the one on Monterosso's **San Cristoforo promontory** (p75), or the more sophisticated bunkers and blockhouses at **La Batterie** (p58) on the Portofino peninsula. Most of the defences were built by the Italians but taken over by the Germans after the 1943 armistice. The Germans also placed an anti-aircraft battery atop Vernazza's historic castle.

Super-Quiet Trails

The Riviera, like much of Italy, is infamous for its summer crowds, but you can enjoy surprising tranquillity if you veer off the main paths onto trails less travelled. Peaceful walks include the **Alta Via delle Cinque Terre** (p70), the trails around Lerici and Tellaro, and the network of old tracks that crisscrosses Genoa's **Parco delle Mura** (p40).

Churches as Art Galleries

While walking around Genoa's tightly-packed *caruggi* (alleyways; p44) you'll stumble upon the wooden doorways of many easy-to-miss churches – not any old churches but cavernous baroque beauties whose interiors are decorated with bright, intricate frescoes. Places worth seeking out include the lavishly embellished **Basilica di San Siro**, the colourful **Chiesa di San Filippo Neri** and vast temple-like **Basilica della Santissima Annunziata del Vastato**, whose gold-rimmed ceiling frescoes are an absolute marvel.

OFFBEAT GENOA & CINQUE TERRE

Genoa's most secretive bar **Malkovich** (p50) is an entry-by-password speak-easy that shakes and stirs superb cocktails.

Slowly being recolonised by nature, the ruins of **Portesone** (p137) are a ghostly antidote to the cute backstreets of nearby Tellaro.

Looking like an injured Hercules carved into the cliffside, Monte-rosso's **Statua del Gigante** (p75) still has the power to turn heads.

Come to Genoa's **Castello d'Albertis** (p43) to see the wild and whimsical collection of former sea captain and world traveller, Enrico Alberto d'Albertis.

GABRIELLE PHOTOGRAPHS/SHUTTERSTOCK ©

Hiking trail, Parco delle Mura (p40)

FABER1893/SHUTTERSTOCK ©

Basilica della Santissima Annunziata del Vastato (p44)

Explore Genoa & Cinque Terre

Genoa & Cinque Terre Walking Tours

Manarola (p109)

See p48
for eating, drinking and shopping listings

Explore Genoa

Shadowy alleys and elegant piazzas, freshly ground pesto and crispy focaccia, wrinkled tenements and palaces vying to outdo each other with their giddy opulence. Welcome to Genoa, the cultural capital of the Italian Riviera, a sprawling port city that once presided over a maritime empire that dominated Mediterranean trade and finance for over 700 years. Gritty and gracious in equal measure, Genoa's legacy is immense. The main draws for modern visitors are its medieval *caruggi* (narrow streets), its simple trattoria food and its remarkable Palazzi Rolli, 42 aristocratic lodging houses dating from the 16th and 17th centuries that harbour world-class art collections. Providing a modern support act are the innovations of the rejuvenated port, including Europe's second-largest aquarium.

Getting Around

Walking

Genoa is mostly walkable, although you should be prepared to get lost temporarily in the hard-to-navigate *caruggi*.

Lifts & Funicular

An ingenious series of elevators and funiculars link the city centre with the hilly neighbourhoods to the north.

Bus

Local buses can deposit you at the beaches abutting the Corso Italia or you can walk along Corso Aurelio Saffi from the Porto Antico (3km).

Metro

There's a single-line subway system that interconnects with the main Piazza Principe train station.

THE BEST

TRATTORIA
Cavour 21 (p48)

CAFE FOR A 'PAUSA'
Marescotti di Cavo (p50)

UNESCO-LISTED PALAZZO
Palazzo Reale (p42)

EVENING STROLL
Passeggiata Anita Garibaldi (p47)

MUSEUM
Galata Museo del Mare (p46)

Inner courtyard, Palazzo Doria-Tursi (p38)
JOHANNESS/SHUTTERSTOCK ©

WALKING TOUR

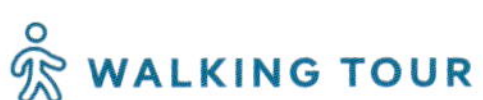

A Walk Around the Porto Antico

Genoa's scimitar-shaped Porto Antico (Old Port) is where the nascent city was first established and where it underwent an ambitious rebuilding project for the 1992 Expo.

START	END	LENGTH
La Lanterna	Palazzo San Giorgio	3½km, 4 hours

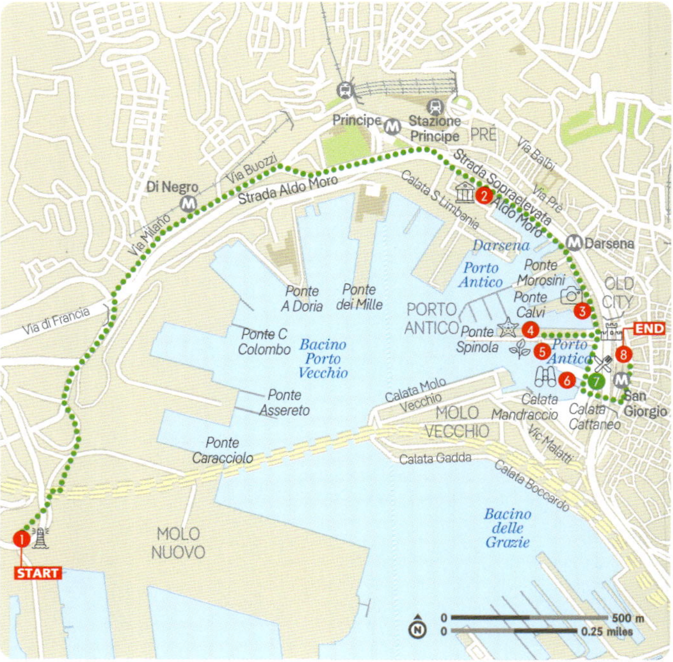

1 La Lanterna

The port may have changed radically since its 1990s rebirth, but its emblematic sentinel hasn't moved an inch since 1543. Genoa's **lighthouse** is one of the world's oldest and tallest – and it still works, beaming its light over 50km to warn ships and tankers. Visitors can climb 172 steps and ponder exhibits in an adjacent museum of lamps, lenses and related history.

2 Museum of the Sea

Follow the curve of the harbour northeast to the **Galata Museo del Mare** (p46) where you can enjoy four floors of superbly curated exhibits in an exhaustive study of Genoa's maritime history with mock-ups of old galleons and galleys.

3 Docked Galleon

Two piers further east is the anchored ship, **Neptuno**, a reproduction of a 17th-century galleon used in films and beloved by kids who get to scamper around the decks.

4 Water World

Nearby, Renzo Piano's 'new port' is anchored by the gigantic **aquarium**, the second-largest in Europe, which protects 400 marine species in 70 tanks, including sharks, dolphins, penguins and seals.

5 Giant Greenhouse

A giant glass orb housing a humid mini-ecosystem with tropical plants, butterflies and birds, the **Biosfera** is an innovative addition to the port, although its assorted greenery probably won't delay you more than 15 minutes. The ambient temperature inside is controlled by computers. It was designed by Renzo Piano in 2001, and is known locally as '*la bolla*' (the bubble).

6 Ride in a Lift

Stroll around the dock to the **Bigo**, a panoramic lift designed to resemble the cranes once used to unload freight from ships.

7 Multiple Flavours

The late-19th-century Millo building was once a busy warehouse and today hosts the equally busy **Eataly** (p51), Italy's delicious food emporium with its affiliated seafood restaurant, Il Marin (p50).

8 Mural-Covered Palace

Palazzo San Giorgio, on Genoa's waterfront, was constructed in 1260. St George is one of Genoa's patron saints, and the dragon slayer is featured prominently underneath the clock. The six men depicted below St George represent some of Genoa's most famous native sons, including Christopher Columbus, second from left.

A
B
C
D
1
2
3
4
5
6
Via Balbi
Via delle Monachette
Via Bellucci
Via Brignole
Corso Carbonara
Palazzo Reale
Basilica della Santissima Annunziata del Vastato
Piazza Carmine
Via Brignole
Vic della Pace
Strada Sopraelevata Aldo Moro
Via Balbi
Piazza Bandiera
Galata Museo del Mare
Via Antonio Gramsci
Via Prè
PRÈ
Calata de Mari
Darsena
Piazza della Annunziata
Largo della Zecca
Via Bensa
Via delle Fontane
Chiesa di San Filippo Neri
Darsena
Via Lomellini
Via Cairoli
Galleria G Garibaldi
Consorzio Liguria Via Mare
Via del Campo
Porto Antico
The Musei di Strada Nuova
Ponte Morosini
Basilica di San Siro
Palazzo Bianco
Palazzo Rosso
Ponte Calvi
Via Morchi
Via della Maddalena
Galleria Nazionale di Palazzo Spinola
Ponte Spinola
Via San Luca
Piazza Caricamento
OLD CITY (CARUGGI)
Bacino Porto Vecchio
Porto Antico
Palazzo San Giorgio
Via Banchi
Via di Soziglia
Vic Neve
Calata Molo Vecchio
Piazzale Luigi Durand de la Pierre
Piazza Campetto
San Giorgio
Vic Indoratori
Calata Cattaneo
Calata Mandraccio
Strada Sopraelevata Aldo Moro
Vic Curto
Piazza San Lorenzo
Cattedrale di San Lorenzo
MOLO VECCHIO
Via di Canneto Il Curto
Via San Lorenzo
Via del Molo
Via di Canneto Il Lungo
Museo del Tesoro
Vic Malatti
Piazza San Marco
CASTELLO
Via dei Giustiniani
Vic delle Vele
Piazza Cavour
Via di San Bernardo
Salita Pollaiuoli
Calata Boccardo
Basilica di Santa Maria di Castello
Via di Mascherona
Via Santa Maria di Castello
Via di S Croce
Piazza Renato Negri
1 2 7 8 9 10 11 13 14 15 16 17
21 22 24 25 27 28 29 31 32 33 36 38 39 41 42 43 44 45 46 47 48 49 50 55 57

For more see
Top Experiences p38
Experiences p43
Eating p48
Drinking p50
Shopping p51
0 200 m
0 0.1 miles
Piazza Golfredo Villa
CASTELLETTO
Spianata Castelletto
Palazzo Doria-Tursi
Piazza del Portello
Piazzale Mazzini
Piazza Marsala
The Ring of Forts
Parco delle Mura (4.5km); Forte Begato, Forte Sperone (5km); Forte Diamante (8.5km)
Piazza delle Fontane Marose
Piazza Corvetto
Spianata dell'Acquasola
Piazza Piccapietra
Teatro Carlo Felice
Palazzo Ducale
De Ferrari
Piazza de Ferrari
Piazza Giacomo Matteotti
Chiesa del Gesù
Palazzo della Borsa
Piazza Portoria
Casa di Colombo
Piazza Dante
Corso Firenze
Corso Paganini
Corso Magenta
Salita S Gerolamo
Via Caffaro
Salita Sant'Anna
Salita Battistina
Galleria N Bixio
Via Piaggio
Via G Mameli
Via Goito
Via Palestro
Corso Solferino
Via G Bertora
Via Assarotti
Via Serra
Via Garibaldi
Via Luccoli
Via XXV Aprile
Via Roma
Galleria Mazzini
Via Cabà
Vic della Casana
Via XII Ottobre
Via Pammat
Via IV Novembre
Via Carcassi
Via E Vernazza
Via XX Settembre
Via V Dicembre
Via San Vincenzo
Via di Porta Soprana
Via Dante
Via Ceccardi
Via Fieschi
Corso Podestà
Via Maragliano
Via Fasella
Via Cesarea
Vic del Fico
Via di Ravecca
EXPLORE
GENOA

★ TOP EXPERIENCE

Musei di Strada Nuova

The Strade Nuove or 'New Streets' is the collective name given to three interconnected thoroughfares that were laid out on the cusp of medieval Genoa in the 16th century. They house three of the most preeminent Palazzi Rolli, constructed between the 1530s and 1670s and redeveloped as a joint museum in 2004.

MAP P36 **D3–E3**

PLANNING TIP
A joint ticket for the three Musei di Strada Nuova costs €9 in person or €10 if you buy it online.

Strade Nuove

The Strade Nuove is the term used to denote Vias Balbi, Cairoli and Garibaldi, the wide streets that were developed in the 16th century to accommodate the Palazzi Rolli. Built and financed by rich Genovese aristocrats, including the Doria, Spinola and Lomellino families, the luxuriant private residences were constructed between the 1530s and 1670s in the prevailing Renaissance and baroque styles, with their interiors elaborately embellished with frescoes and stucco.

Palazzo Bianco

Flemish, Spanish and Italian artists are on show at Palazzo Bianco, the oldest of the 'big three' Rolli palaces built between 1530 and 1540 by the aristocratic Grimaldi family. Today, it brings together Genoa's finest collection of Old Masters. Caravaggio's *Ecce Homo*, Rubens' *Venere e Marte (Venus and Mars)* and Van Dyck's *Vertumno e Pomona* play a starring role, but there are also works by Hans Memling, Filippino Lippi and Spanish baroque painters.

Palazzo Doria-Tursi

This largest of the Rolli palaces also serves as Genoa's town hall and visitors are free to wander around the courtyard and admire the outdoor terraces and grandiose staircases.

Scan for prices and opening hours.

TRABANTOS/SHUTTERSTOCK ©

Of particular interest in the onsite museum is the collection of legendary Genovese violinist Niccolò Paganini's personal effects, including his 'Cannone' *(cannon)* violin, made in Cremona in 1743 and named for its powerful tone. One lucky musician gets to play it during October's Paganini festival.

Palazzo Rosso

Arguably the most quintessential of the Palazzi Rolli, the Rosso (pictured) was a latecomer to the ball. Built in the 1670s, too late to be included on the original 'lists', its lavishly frescoed rooms provide a striking backdrop for works by Van Dyck, Guido Reni, Guercino, Dürer and Bernardo Strozzi. Restoration work in 2022 resurrected a ceiling fresco by Gregorio de Ferrari in the Sala della Primavera, while an avant-garde suite of apartment rooms, located on an upper-floor mezzanine, includes an unusual grotto hall and a lavish alcove bedroom.

QUICK BREAK

The Palazzo Rosso has its own cafe-restaurant known as **Mentelocale** ('Local Mind', p50) offering coffee, snacks and an afternoon aperitif buffet.

★ TOP EXPERIENCE

The Ring of Forts

Lying within easy reach of the city centre, courtesy of a funicular railway, this extensive nature park contains the well-preserved ruins of several forts. A visit to its lofty confines provides an intriguing insight into Genoa's erstwhile role as a maritime power.

MAP P36 **H3**

PLANNING TIP
Load up with focaccia and panini in Genoa and come prepared for a picnic beside one of the hilltop ruins. There are several designated picnic areas.

Scan for information on Parco delle Mura.

A Defensive Network

As a powerful city state, Genoa historically sought protection behind a formidable system of walls and forts built and rebuilt in various guises from the 9th century onwards. The most ambitious bastions, the so-called 'New Walls', were constructed between 1626 and 1639 on the high ridges that surround the city on its landward side. At their peak, they stretched for 20km and were punctuated with numerous hilltop forts. Several of the structures remain intact and can be explored on foot on an easy day trip from Genoa.

Exploring the Forts

Start by taking a 10-minute funicular ride from Zecca in the city centre up to the hilly suburb of Righi from where a paved road continues further uphill into the **Parco delle Mura**, a protected area dotted with half a dozen forts that can be incorporated into a three-hour circular hike.

The first fort, **Castellaccio**, has a small cafe built into a roadside arch and makes a good refreshment stop and orientation point. From here, it's a short walk on a paved road to **Forte Begato** and **Forte Sperone** (pictured), two well-preserved citadels dating from the 1820s. Continuing on a path north along a ridge from Sperone you'll pass privately owned Forte Puin before coming into sight of the

COLLECTION MAYKOVA/SHUTTERSTOCK ©

imposing walls of **Diamante** (1756), the most outlying of the forts that sits splendidly atop a 667m-high hill like an enchanted castle.

Hiking Country

All the forts are currently closed to the public and are in varying states of repair. However, you can get up close enough to touch their historic walls and enjoy superb vistas of the surrounding hills and ridges along with eagle-eye views of Genoa splayed below. The hiking trails are equally alluring, meandering through a mix of sun-dappled woodland and open grassland abundant with butterflies in summer.

The Ferrovia Genova-Casella

There are spectacular views of Genoa's forts from this 1929 **narrow-gauge railway**, which snakes 25km north from the cute Stazione di Genova Piazza to Trensacaso, where a trail heads west to Forte Diamante.

QUICK BREAK

The **Ostaia du Richetto** (p51) is a simple cafe/restaurant encased in an old tower that arches over the road at the entrance to the Parco delle Mura.

★ TOP EXPERIENCE

Palazzo Reale

A former residence of the Savoy dynasty, the Palazzo Reale is Genoa's proverbial Versailles with terraced gardens, exquisite furnishings, a fine collection of 17th-century Genovese art and a gilded Hall of Mirrors eerily redolent of its French counterpart. It is, arguably, the city's most emblematic building.

MAP P36 **B1**

PLANNING TIP
If you plan to visit Musei di Strada Nuova and other sites around Genoa, it's worth investing in the **Card Musei di Genova** (Genoa Museum Card), which gives access to over 25 city museums.

History of the Palace

Built by the Balbi family in the 1640s and passed on to the Durazzo clan in 1677, the Palazzo Reale was ultimately purchased by the House of Savoy in 1824 and went on to become a summer residence for the king. The Emanuele clan renovated various rooms, creating a throne room, audience chamber and ball room among other refittings. It remained a royal residence until 1919, when King Vittorio Emanuele III ceded it to the Italian State.

Rooms & Paintings

The grandeur of this noble residence is apparent as you ascend the stairs and wander through a series of elaborately decorated rooms. Through these no-expense-spared chambers you'll find a mix of oversized oil paintings, lavish stucco details, Classical marble sculptures, Flemish tapestries and dazzling ceiling frescoes.

Gardens & Exterior

To get a better view of the scale and opulence of the palace, step into the rear gardens where its tall terracotta facade rises above an intricate garden designed in the style of a Roman nymphaeum. A central pond is surrounded by a haunting pebble mosaic best viewed from the terraces above.

Scan for more information on the palace.

EXPERIENCES

See Where Columbus Grew Up MUSEUM

MAP: 1 P36 **E6**

Talk about humble beginnings. The man responsible for linking two great continents and, inadvertently, putting tomatoes in your pizza was born in Genoa in 1451. Take this tiny abode and its onsite museum *(museidigenova.it; tickets €3)* with a pinch of salt: **Casa di Colombo** is a reconstruction of the original house where Columbus lived hereabouts between 1455 and 1470, with some brief but intriguing details of the great navigator's life and journeys. Curiously, it stands just outside the old city walls in the shadow of the fort-like Porta Soprana gate built in 1155.

Investigate the Eclectic Castello d'Albertis MUSEUM

MAP: 2 P36 **A1**

Dating from the late 1880s, this neo-Gothic Xanadu in the Castelletto neighbourhood was built to resemble a castle by Italian navigator, writer and philanthropist Enrico d'Albertis. Its **museum** *(museidigenova.it; adult/child €6/4.50)* houses a wide array of ethnographic artefacts from around the globe amassed by D'Albertis during his many travels.

The bright galleries cover the map from pre-Colombian pottery to installations exploring traditional medicines of the Far East. A leafy terrace by the entrance offers fine views over the city. The castle is a short steep climb from Stazione Piazza Principe, or you can save your legs by taking the Ascensore Montegalletto.

Pause in the Piazza de Ferrari SQUARE

Easily Genoa's grandest square, bright **Piazza de Ferrari** (MAP: 3 P36 **E5**), with its graceful fountain, offers visual relief for visitors emerging from the confines of the *caruggi*. It's bordered by a ring of prestigious buildings including the neo-Grecian **Teatro Carlo Felice** (MAP: 4 P36 **E5**; *operacarlofelicegenova.it*) – check its website for upcoming opera performances; the neoclassical **Palazzo Ducale** (MAP: 5 P36 **E5**; *palazzoducale.genova.it; adult/child €14/8)*, host to international-caliber exhibitions; and the **Palazzo della Borsa**, (MAP: 6 P36 **E5**) former home of the city's stock exchange.

There are several cafes where you can enjoy an elongated '*pausa*'.

The Genovese Trattoria Experience FOOD

Prego. Take a seat at a wobbly wooden table, peruse a hastily scribbled blackboard menu and grab a hunk of fresh bread from the generously filled basket that gets plonked down at your table before you've even had a chance to pull up a chair. Welcome to the intriguing world of Genovese

THE NUANCES OF PESTO

It would be criminal to come to Genoa and not try *pesto genovese.* The city's famous raw pasta sauce is made from a pounded mix of young basil leaves (grown locally), untoasted pine nuts, extra-virgin olive oil, cheese (a mixture of *parmigiano reggiano* and *pecorino*), salt and a very small measure of uncooked garlic. If you want to be really exacting, you should grind the ingredients by hand with a pestle and mortar made from Carrara marble. The result is an earthy, deliciously fragrant sauce made using techniques honed through generations.

trattorias, the cherished crucibles of what Italians call *cucina casalinga* (home cooking); delicious, simple, unembellished local fare that arrives at your table faster than a Big Mac but harks back to a food culture that's been around for centuries.

All serve the hallowed classics of Genovese cooking: trofie with pesto, *pansotti* (herb-filled ravioli) and walnut sauce, *corniglio* (rabbit) *ragù, farinata* (chickpea pancakes), vegetable pies and anchovies done multiple ways. The *caruggi* hide the best of the crop, particularly the southeastern section around Piazza Cavour. Try Trattoria delle Grazie (p48) or join the queue outside Cavour 21 (p48).

Get Disorientated in the Caruggi — HISTORIC QUARTER

Many Italian cities are crisscrossed by dark medieval streets, but none are as labyrinthine as Genoa's. The famous *caruggi* comprise a hard-to-navigate web of twisting lanes and sun-starved alleys – some so narrow that residents can literally lean out and fist-bump their neighbours across the street. For visitors, it's practically impossible to follow any prearranged itinerary; instead, succumb to spontaneous adventure as you dip into noisy trattorias and niche century-old shops before finding yourself in a cramped piazza adorned with an frescoed church or an ornate palace.

Places worth lingering in this close-knit, tightly coiled quarter include **Piazza Campetto** (MAP: 7 P36 **D4**) whose palaces have been turned into boho bars and shops; the **Basilica di San Siro** (MAP: 8 P36 **D3**), whose classical facade obscures a dazzlingly baroque interior; colourful **Chiesa di San Filippo Neri** (MAP: 9 P36 **C2**) and temple-like **Basilica della Santissima Annunziata del Vastato** (MAP: 10 P36 **C2**).

The Caffè degli Specchi (p50) is where Italian poet Dino Campana once knocked back espressos while scribbling his elegiac musings.

Find Time for the National Gallery — GALLERY

MAP: 11 P36 **D3**

Included on Palazzo Reale's entry ticket is the Palazzo Spinola di Pellicceria, located in the *caruggi,* which houses Genoa's **Galleria Nazionale di Palazzo Spinola** *(museidigenova.it; adult/reduced €10/6).* This national gallery wonderfully displayes Italian and Flemish Renaissance paintings from the so-called Ligurian School over four floors. Look out for Rubens' Herculean *Portrait of Giovanni Carlo Doria on Horseback.* The architecture, including a ceiling fresco depicting the Siege of Lisbon by Lazzaro Tavarone, is equally majestic.

Take an Elevator to Spianata Castelletto VIEWPOINT

MAP: 12 P36 **E2**

Once outside the city but now very much inside it, this superb **viewpoint** is a short, steep walk or quick elevator ride from Via Garibaldi. The broad *spianata* (esplanade) at the top is lined by palms and reveals the natural amphitheatre of Genoa in all its glory clustered around its harbour. A once-sturdy *castelletto* (little castle) was removed in the 19th century. This being Italy, even the art-nouveau lifts (of which there are two) are beautiful.

Explore One of Italy's Most Unusual Cathedrals CHURCH

Even if you've had your fill of Italian churches, Genoa's **Cattedrale di San Lorenzo** (MAP: 13 P36 **D5**) deserves a detailed examination. A curious mix of two competing architectural styles, Romanesque and Gothic, it owes its continued existence to the poor quality of a British bomb that failed to ignite in 1941 after being fired from a ship in the harbour. The offending projectile is displayed on the right side of the nave like a macabre museum exhibit. Fronted by Gothic portals, twisting columns and crouching lions, the cathedral was consecrated in 1118 but mostly rebuilt in the 1300s. The two bell towers and cupola were added in the 16th century.

The dark Romanesque interior with its zebra-striped columns is brightened by dramatic frescoes by Lazzaro Tavarone above the altar. Tavarone also painted the

RUBENS IN GENOA

Sometimes referred to as the father of baroque, Flemish painter Peter Paul Rubens was a hugely influential artist who was inspired by the work of Titian and Caravaggio to create dramatic, colourful and full-bodied paintings that went on to influence the likes of Van Dyck, Strozzi and the emerging Genovese school. In the early 1600s, he spent nearly a decade roaming Italy, much of it in Genoa, where he gained commissions from the city's most powerful and wealthy families for whom he painted numerous striking portraits. Rubens left a big impact on many paintings in Genoa, including two notable religious works in the **Chiesa del Gesù**.

BERNARDO STROZZI

If you only have time to learn about one artist from the distinguished Genovese school, make sure it's **Bernardo Strozzi** (1581–1644). A former friar at a Capuchin monastery in Genoa, Strozzi's early paintings were mainly religious in nature, influenced by the prevailing Mannerist aesthetic. After being exposed to Caravaggio in the 1610s, Strozzi developed a more naturalistic style characterised by bold colour, contrasting light and rich sensuality. Towards the end of his career, he began painting genre scenes and still life inspired by Flemish artists active in Genoa such as Rubens and Van Dyck.

haunting *Last Supper* mounted in the right nave. The sacristy guards the **Museo del Tesoro** (MAP: 14 P36 **D5**; *museidigenova.it; adult/child €5/4)*, an unlikely treasure box that preserves several holy relics of questionable provenance, including the medieval 'Sacro Catino', a glass vessel once thought to be the Holy Grail.

Enjoy a Maritime Museum par Excellence

MUSEUM

MAP: 15 P36 **A2**

Genoa was a Renaissance and medieval maritime power rivalled only by Barcelona and Venice, meaning its **Galata Museo del Mare** *(galatamuseodelmare.it; adult/reduced €17/14)* is one of the most relevant and interesting museums of its type in Europe. High-tech exhibits trace the history of seafaring, from Genoa's reign as the continent's greatest dockyard to the ages of sail and steam.

A section on the ground floor is dedicated to native son Christopher Columbus. Alongside is a scale reconstruction of a 17th-century galley ship, given extra drama by sound effects and snippets of film.

The 2nd floor guards a valuable collection of old maps and globes, while the 3rd floor has a more recent documentation of Italian emigration by sea. The top-floor mirador has one of Genoa's best portside views.

Uncover Genoa's Forgotten Church

CHURCH

MAP: 16 P36 **C6**

Genoa's *caruggi* are stuffed with elaborately decorated churches that give very away little from the outside. One of the oldest and most consistently overlooked is the Romanesque **Basilica di Santa Maria di Castello** *(santamariadicastello.it)* and its convent, built before 900 CE, with its walls covered with treasures commissioned by the noble families of Genoa from the earliest times.

There are also notable frescoes from 16th and 17th century. Fabulous onsite guides will impart the building's history.

Go Whale-Watching on the Riviera

WILDLIFE TOUR

MAP: 17 P36 **B3**

Observing nature's largest mammals might not be the first thing visitors associate with Genoa, but the experience of whale-watching – on a good day – could leave one of the deepest impressions. The Pelagos sanctuary is a diamond-shaped tract of the Mediterranean between Sardinia, Tuscany and the Ligurian coast that is protected as a marine area. It supports a healthy population of striped dolphins, turtles, seabirds, and pilot, sperm and fin whales.

Consorzio Liguria Via Mare *(liguriaviamare.it; tours adult/child €42/25)* offers five-hour tours run in consultation with the WWF, which include fascinating background on the marine mammals provided by an onboard marine biologist. Their 160-seat vessel is wheelchair accessible and departs from Genoa's Porto Antico.

Imbibe Sundowners in Boccadasse

NEIGHBOURHOOD

MAP: 18 P36 **G6**

When the day starts to wane, do as the Genovese do and join in the *passeggiata* (late-afternoon stroll) along the oceanside promenade, Corso Italia, which begins around 3km east of Genoa's city centre. This broad 2.5km-long pavement lined with extravagant villas and expensive beach clubs terminates at **Boccadasse**, a once-separate fishing village that glimmers like an outlying member of Cinque Terre. Its sheltered beach is perfect gelato-licking territory, and its bars are an ideal spot to chink glasses as the sun says goodnight.

Continue Genoa's Art History in Nervi

MUSEUM

MAP: 19 P36 **H6**

The Genoa suburb of Nervi has a quartet of art museums worthy of a day-trip. Of the four, the **Galleria d'Arte Moderna** *(museidigenova.it; joint ticket €8)* set in the 17th-century Villa Saluzzo, is the numero uno. Acting as an epilogue to the baroque works amassed in Genoa's Palazzi Rolli, it displays the collection of the former Prince Odone di Savoia, including works by 19th- and early-20th-century artists such as futurist Fortunato Depero, semi-official fascist sculptor Arturo Martini and the lyrical, eccentric Filippo De Pisis.

Join the Passeggiata

WALKWAY

MAP: 20 P36 **H6**

Nervi's 2km-long promenade, the **Passeggiata Anita Garibaldi**, is a strong contender for the best afternoon stroll in Liguria. An elevated terracotta pathway that's nailed to the rocky shoreline, it zigzags between headlands and narrow coves where Italian sunbathers lay out their towels wherever they can find a flat rock. Don't miss the old watchtower converted into an art gallery.

LISTINGS

Best Places for...

€ Budget €€ Midrange €€€ Top End

Eating

Traditional Genovese Trattorias

Cavour 21 €
21 C6
Long queues, fast service and quick turnover characterise this hole-in-the-wall by the old port. Of note is the hearty *corniglio* (rabbit *ragù*). *noon-2.30pm & 7-10.30pm*

Trattoria delle Grazie €
22 C5
Sit alfresco in a narrow city alleyway and enjoy the delights of *mandilli* pesto (with lasagne-like noodles), anchovies and *pansotti* (herb-filled ravioli) in walnut sauce. *12.30-2pm & 7.30-9.30pm Thu-Tue*

Trattoria da Maria €
23 F4
Lightning-fast lunches of unadorned Genovese *cibo* (street food) accompanied by jugs of wine and mountains of bread. Opt for the minestrone soup. *11.45am-2.45pm Mon-Sat, 6.15-10pm Thu & Fri*

Osteria di Vico Palla €
24 B5
Known for its stewed stockfish with potatoes olives and pesto, the Vico down by the port is so old, 17th-century Flemish painter Van Dyck used to stop by for his evening repast. *noon-3pm & 7.30-10.45pm Tue-Sun*

Trattoria della Raibetta €€
25 C5
A snug trattoria with a low brick-vaulted ceiling that serves *trofiette al pesto* the proper way (with green beans and potato) along with octopus salad, fresh fish and superb chocolate-cake desserts. *noon-2pm & 7.30-10pm Tue-Sun*

Trattoria Rosmarino €€
26 E5
More upmarket than your average trattoria, Rosmarino merits a romantic dinner of down-to-earth food near the Piazza de Ferrari. *12.30-2.30pm & 7.30-10.30pm Mon-Sat*

Giardino degli Indoratori €€
27 D5
Squeeze onto a laneway table in the *caruggi* or recline in a cosy, monochrome dining room as you contemplate seafood and seasonal vegetable *primi* – from linguine to gnocchi and risotto to filled pastas. Sign off with a heavenly pistachio tiramisu for dessert. *noon-3pm & 7-11pm Mon-Sat, 7-11pm Sun*

Pizza From Genuine to Gourmet

Pizzeria Savô €€
28 C3
Gourmet pizza in Italy might seem like an oxymoron but, while the pizzas at Savô are undoubtedly fancy by local standards, they live up to their billing with top-quality produce and fresh green flourishes. *noon-2.30pm & 7-10.30pm Mon-Fri, 7-10.30pm Sat & Sun*

I Tre Merli €€
29 C5
If you don't mind a bit of tourist company and are after a wide-choice menu that covers everything from cheeseburgers to wood-fired pizzas and focaccia, head down to the old port where the 'Three Blackbirds' is encased in the 19th-century Millio building next door to Eataly. *12.10-3pm & 7.30-11pm*

Creative Meat Dishes

Matamà €€
30 H6
A Nervi meat specialist serving steak, ribs, stew and pasta in a bistro-like interior near the Porticiollo. The alternating menu includes Wagyu, Bourguignonne, and Argentinian entrecote, all of which pairs well with a glass of port. *7.30pm-midnight Wed-Mon*

Street Food

Antica Trattoria Sà Pesta €
31 C5
A landmark trattoria serving classic Genovese *farinata* (chickpea flour flatbread) made in seasoned antique pans in a wood-fired oven out front. *noon-2pm Mon-Wed, noon-2pm & 7-8.45pm Thu-Sat*

Focaccia e Dintorni €
32 C5
Arguably the most beloved focacceria in Genoa as long, semi-permanent queues outside will testify. Come and savour the aroma of fresh Italian bread baked all day long. *7am-8pm*

La Focacceria di Teobaldo €
 B1
Serves up wide variety of focaccia slices a short stroll from the Stazione Principe. Great for grabbing a snack while waiting for your train. *8am-7pm Mon-Sat*

Mercato Orientale Genova €
 H6
A gourmet Italian food hall in the middle of the city's primary produce market with over a dozen diverse eating options and well-scrubbed communal tables at which to enjoy them. Everything from Japanese to Peruvian cuisine is represented. *10am-11pm Mon-Sat*

Rooster €
 E5
A cute little hole-in-the-wall next to the cathedral that breathes new life into traditional rotisserie chicken, serving it in everything from poke bowls to sandwiches and salads. *10.30am-10pm*

Friggitoria San Giorgio €
 C4
In Genoa, fish and chips entails a paper cone filled with deep-fried squid and embellished with chips made from chickpea batter. San Giorgio is a longstanding portside favourite. *11am-9pm*

Gelato

Gelateria Profumo €
37 E4
A wonderfully old-fashioned gelato parlour in the midst of the *caruggi* with fragrant scoops of unusual flavours including Sorrento lemon and bitter orange. *noon-7pm Tue-Sat*

La Cremeria delle Erbe €
 D6
On agreeably shabby Piazza delle Erbe, this feted gelateria snares late-night diners and boozers with generous scoops of occasionally lurid flavours. *11am-1am*

Vegetarian

Soul Kitchen €€

39 C3

A rarity in fish-loving Genova, the vegetarian-friendly Soul Kitchen emits a psychedelic vibe while knocking out uncompromising non-meat/fish classics like pesto, *pansotti* in walnut sauce, spaghetti Nerano (courgettes) and arancini. *12.30-3pm & 7.30-11pm Wed-Sun*

Seafood

Trattoria Osvaldo €€

40 G6

Obligatory seafood stop, a few steps up from the water in the fishing village turned Genovese suburb of Boccadasse. Grilled octopus, stockfish and prawns with fettucine all feature prominently. *12.30-2pm & 7.30-10.30pm Thu-Sun*

Il Marin €€€

41 C5

Italian food store Eataly's 3rd-floor fine-dining space emits an easy, relaxed glamour, while dishes use unusual Mediterranean-sourced produce and look gorgeous on the plate. It's Michelin-starred, so book ahead. *7.30-10pm Wed-Fri & Mon, 12.30-2pm & 7.30-10pm Sat & Sun*

Soho €€€

42 C3

Both a restaurant and fishmonger, Soho is the place to come for the raw stuff. Try the 'maxi' *crudite di mare* plate – a mermaid-like feast of raw fish and seafood. *noon-11pm*

Light Lunch

Mentelocale €€

43 B1

There are several of these studious cafes encased in Genoa's Rolli palaces, but this particular branch in the Palazzo Reale is arguably the best place to interrupt your museum musings with coffee, cake and sandwiches in exquisite surroundings. *7.30am-7.30pm*

Drinking

Bohemian Drinking Dens

Les Rouges

44 D4

Crumbling frescoed *palazzo* reborn as atmospheric cocktail bar in the claustrophobic Piazza Campetto offering potent drinks with herbal and floral ingredients. *6-11.45pm Sun-Thu, to 12.45am Fri & Sat*

La Nouvelle Vague

45 D5

Trendy underground hub of drinks, books, cool people, decent food and live music close to the cathedral. *6pm-1am*

Malkovich

46 D3

Tucked under the trendy burger joint Groove, Malkovich serves Genoa's best cocktails. Entry is via password only. *9pm-1am*

Scurreria Beer & Bagel

see 27 D5

A *caruggi* brewpub with over a dozen taps of beer and a nice sideline in stuffed bagels. *6pm-1am Mon-Fri, from noon Sat & Sun*

Cafes to Linger In

Caffè degli Specchi

47 D5

Mirrored art-deco showpiece in the old town where you can imbibe espresso and/or *aperitivi* while admiring your reflection in the glass. It's been holding court on this street corner since 1908. *8am-9.30pm*

Marescotti di Cavo

48 C3

Grand old dowager of a cafe in the *caruggi* with coffee and sweet pastries served at frisbee-sized street tables or on the marble counter inside. *7.30am-7.30pm*

Cafhein

A1

Modern cafe near Piazza Principe station serving sandwiches, cakes and drip coffee. There's free wi-fi and space to hunker down with a laptop inside. *7.30am-7pm*

Cairoli Cafe

D2

Popular place for a coffee break or a lunchtime snack on the Strada Nuova in the heart of Genoa's museum district. *7am-7.30pm*

Eataly

see 41 **C5**

On the ground floor of Italy's famous food emporium in the Porto Antico, this mega-popular cafe serves a reliable selection of high-quality coffee, pastries and sandwiches. *10am-10pm*

Beers & Aperitifs

Bar Berto

E6

The heart of the *caruggi*'s boozy nightlife is Piazza delle Erbe – more a misshapen rectangle than a square – where the alfresco tables of no-nonsense Bar Berto merge with a clutch of others. *10am-1am*

Ostaia du Richetto

H3

If you're up in the delightfully rural Parco delle Mura, this small bar and snack joint built into the wall of one of the old forts is a good place to wind up post-hike for a coffee or beer. *9am-10pm Fri-Wed*

Shopping

Fashion & Furniture

Via Garibaldi 12

53 **E3**

Reserve time to climb the stairs of Palazzo Baldassarre Lomellini in Via Garibaldi to peruse the artsy offerings in Genoa's chicest and most expensive furniture shop. *10am-2pm & 3.30-7pm Tue-Sat*

Temide

54 **E4**

Small *caruggi* boutique that sells works by local artists and artisans, including delicate ceramics, ornate jewellery and hand-painted silk scarves. *10.30am-2pm & 3.30-7.30pm Tue-Sat, 3.30-7.30pm Mon*

Paccottiglia

D5

Whimsical concept store with a trove of thoughtfully curated garments and one-of-a-kind accessories including soft cotton shirts, espadrilles, bath products, canvas bags, blank notebooks and curious wall art. *10.30am-1.30pm & 3.30-7.30pm Tue-Sat*

Books & Chocolate

Feltrinelli Librerie

56 **F6**

The Genoa branch of Italy's fabulous book emporium is a dreamy place. Spread over several floors, it stocks multi-lingual literature, travel guides, stationery, music and kid's toys. A bibliophile's paradise. *9am-8pm Mon-Sat, to 8pm Sun*

Pietro Romanengo fu Stefano

D4

A historic chocolate shop (established 1780) that specialises in candied flowers and floral waters. The furnishings, including marble floor, frescoed ceiling and rosewood counters, are as colourful as the chocolates themselves. *9am-1pm & 3.15-7.30pm Tue-Sat, 3.30-7.30pm Mon*

See p67
for eating, drinking and shopping listings

Explore
Portofino to Levanto

The segment of the Riviera Levante from Portofino stretching east to Levanto is usually known as the Gulf of Tigullio, after an ancient Ligurian tribe called the Tigulli. This is the Riviera at its most refined and stylish, spearheaded by the chic resort-village of Portofino, a place so popular that, in 2023, it introduced 'no waiting zones' designed to discourage tourists from taking selfies. For a quieter time, take to the coastal trails above Portofino protected in a regional park. Tracking east along the coast, the swankiness continues through Santa Margherita Ligure and Rapallo where large hotels resemble opulent palaces. More down to earth are Camogli and Levanto at either end of the gulf. The former is a still-active fishing community, the latter a small beach town with surfable waves.

Getting Around

Train

Camogli, Santa Margherita Ligure, Rapallo Sestri Levante and Levanto are all interconnected on the main east–west train line with regular services to Genoa, La Spezia and everywhere in between.

Bus

Bus 792 connects from Santa Margherita station to Portofino. The fare is €5.

Boat

Regular boats ferry between Rapallo, Santa Margherita Ligure, Portofino and San Fruttuoso.

Walking

There are sidewalks linking Santa Margherita Ligure with both Portofino and Rapallo.

Portofino
OLENA ZNAK/SHUTTERSTOCK ©

THE BEST

BEACH
San Fruttuoso (p56)

CROWD AVOIDANCE
Parco Naturale Regionale di Portofino (p58)

COASTAL PATH
San Fruttuoso to Portofino (p58)

GLASS OF WINE
Winterose (p69)

FOCACCIA
Revello (p68)

PORTOFINO TO CAVI
For more see
Top Experiences p55
Experiences p60
Eating p67
Drinking p69
Shopping p69
Recco
Camogli
Sagra del Pesce
A12
Rapallo Cable Car
Rapallo
Montallegro
Santuario Basilica di Montallegro
Lungomare Vittorio Veneto
Santa Margherita Ligure
Villa Durazzo
Parco Naturale Regionale di Portofino
Abbazia di San Fruttuoso
San Fruttuoso
SP227
Paraggi
La Portofinese
Spiaggia di Paraggi
See Portofino
Zoagli
Chiavari
Lavagna
Cavi
5 km
2.5 miles
Portofino
Parco Naturale Regionale di Portofino
Vico Dritto
Via Roma
Via Duca degli Abruzzi
Piazzetta
Calata Marconi
Caffè Excelsior
Ligurian Sea
Molo Umberto I
Salita San Giorgio
Castello Brown

★ TOP EXPERIENCE

Rapallo Cable Car

While Genoa employs elevators and funiculars to negotiate its hilly terrain, Rapallo utilises the Funivia Rapallo–Montallegro, a cable car dating from 1934 that ascends 612m from the city centre to the revered Santuario Basilica di Montallegro, a pilgrimage site surrounded by deciduous forest.

MAP P54 **C2**

The Basilica

The basilica stands on a hillside on the spot where, in 1557, the Virgin Mary was purportedly sighted by a local farmer who'd lain down for a nap. Way larger than most Italian sanctuaries, the current structure is an imposing Gothic building with a boldly symmetrical marble facade that dates from 1896. It stands atop a grand staircase that leads up from the cable-car station.

PLANNING TIP
The upper cable-car station has a small cafe, but you'll get better food and views in the hotel restaurant higher up in front of the church.

Ex-Votos & Icons

The elaborate interior contains numerous *ex-votos* (gifts for graces received) the oldest dating from 1574, and the church's most precious object – a wooden tablet depicting the Virgin, supposedly of Byzantine origin. The revered Madonna of Montallegro has been attributed with many miracles, from repelling medieval plagues to causing Allied bombers to miss their targets in World War II.

Pilgrim's Climb

You can hike to the sanctuary on the so-called 'Pilgrim's Climb', a wide cobbled 3km-long path from Rapallo that ascends through mixed woodland to the summit. The views of Rapallo with the Portofino peninsula in the background are sensational. The path starts on Via Don Giovanni Minzoni near the seafront.

Scan for details about cable-car tickets.

★ TOP EXPERIENCE

Abbazia di San Fruttuoso

This tiny boat-in beach, backed by a weighty 10th-century abbey and cut off from the road network by the rugged cliffs of the Portofino promontory, is an open secret among tourists with a little under-the-radar knowledge and consequently gets its fair share of summer day-trippers.

MAP P54 **B3**

PLANNING TIP
Info centres in Santa Margherita and Camogli (both on the train line) give out free walking maps of Portofino's regional 'natural' park. All the trails are clearly signposted.

Scan for information about boats to San Fruttuoso.

The Abbey

The Romanesque abbey dates from the 10th century and contains the relics of San Fructuoso, a martyred Catalan bishop brought here in the 8th century by Greek monks. With its two-tier cloister and octagonal bell tower, it's well worth the €9 entry fee. The abbey is overlooked by a defensive watchtower built by the eminent Genovese Doria family in the 16th century, whose members are buried in the church crypt.

The Statue Beneath the Sea

The seabed just off San Fruttuoso is home to the **Cristo degli Abissi**, a bronze statue depicting Jesus Christ, arms outstretched, standing 17m beneath the surface of the water. It was put there in 1954 by the Italian navy as a homage to divers who had perished at sea. In the years since, the 2.5m-tall Cristo has become a favoured underwater lure for scuba divers and snorkellers, many of whom kayak or paddleboard 300m from San Fruttuoso's beach to see it. It's a relatively easy dive, but best organised under the supervision of a certified Regione Liguria guide. If you're not into getting wet, there's a replica of the statue in San Fruttuoso's abbey.

GUIDO NICORA/SHUTTERSTOCK ©

The Beach

Access to most of San Fruttuoso's beach is free and the sea water is crystal clear. There's a private beach club if you'd prefer to hire a sun-lounger and umbrella (pictured).

Boat or Hike?

The vast majority of visitors arrive on passenger boats from the nearby towns of Camogli or Santa Margherita, while the more adventurous opt to hike in. If you're brave (and not averse to a little exposure) take the coastal trail from Camogli via La Batterie, a WWII gun emplacement, that incorporates the infamous Paso de Baccio cliff traverse (graded 'expert only'). For a less vertiginous experience, you can hike in from Camogli on an alternative route via Toca and Piertre Strette (7km) or from Portofino via the wooded Base 'O' trail (around 4km).

QUICK BREAK

Lurking behind the beach is a basic cafe and a couple of semi-alfresco restaurants. **La Cantina** (p67), in a secluded cove to the east of the main bay, offers superb seafood.

★ TOP EXPERIENCE

Parco Naturale Regionale di Portofino

The Portofino peninsula's 60km worth of narrow trails are a different universe to the sinuous, sports-car-lined road from Santa Margherita Ligure. Many of them are blissfully remote and all are free of charge. Here, rugged coastal cliffs are interspersed with beechwoods and olive groves.

MAP P54 **B3**

PLANNING TIP
The trail network is meticulously signposted. Notwithstanding, tourist offices in Camogli, Portofino and Santa Margherita give out excellent free maps.

Scan for more information on the regional park.

San Rocco & Punta Chiappa

The town of Camogli is a major gateway to the park. A paved path marked by two red dots leads south up 800 steps to the hamlet of San Rocco (pictured). Here, your options widen. You can head inland to Monte di Portofino, descend to the coast at Punta Chiappa, or tackle a tricky cliff traverse at Passo di Baccio. Punta Chiappa is an exposed rocky outcrop on the Portofino promontory's southwest tip where you can swim and sunbathe like an Italian. By sea it's a five-minute boat ride from Camogli, by land a 3km walk via San Rocco.

Monte di Portofino

The park's highest point is Monte di Portofino (610m) whose summit is known as Semaforo Vecchio. Here, a grassy field surrounded by trees is overlooked by a refuge built as a semaphore station by Napoleon's troops in 1807. It was later converted into a telegraph station, but in 1880 a newer facility, Semaforo Nuovo, was constructed lower down the mountain at a much better viewpoint. Follow the signposts via Toca to get here.

Coastal Path to Portofino

The Camogli–Portofino path (two red dots) continues past San Rocco, passing La Batterie, a set of WWII emplacements built by the Italian army in 1941 and taken over by the Germans in 1943. Beyond this, the trail threads vertiginously around the Passo di Baccio, a short, exposed traverse across a cliff-face with only a metal chain for support. Reminiscent of a *via ferrata* (a trail with permanent cables and ladders), it is recommended for expert hikers only (an alternative route goes via Toca). The path then descends to San Fruttuoso's abbey before ascending again and meandering along steep coastal escarpments to the hamlets of Prato and Olmi. The final descent into Portofino is one of the most heavenly walks in Italy (steep steps be damned!).

From Portofino, you can hike along the coast to Santa Margherita Ligure (where trains connect to Genoa, Camogli and Cinque Terre) or take a hillier route via the hamlet of Nozarego.

QUICK BREAK
Slide into the tight, yacht-like interior of **Ü Caban** (p69), a wine bar overlooking Portofino's Piazzetta, and enjoy a charcuterie board complemented by wine produced on a local eco-farm.

EXPERIENCES

Strike a Pose in Portofino's Piazzetta

SQUARE

MAP: 1 P54 **D2**

Even the trees are beautiful in Portofino, a diminutive fishing village turned celebrity haunt nestled amid steep coastal hills in an attractive natural park. Sure, it's expensive and posh, and more than a little pretentious, but anyone who isn't bowled over by Portofino's chic charm and knockout good looks probably needs to check they've still got a pulse.

Portofino's biggest poseurs usually hang out in the **Piazzetta**, a harbourside square ringed by some of Italy's most expensive bars and restaurants (€8 cappuccinos anyone?) where it's customary to kick back with an Aperol *spritz* at tables where Humphrey Bogart and Marcello Mastroianni once held court. For crowd avoidance arrive before 9am for a *caffè* or linger after 5pm.

Behold Handsome Views from Castello Brown

CASTLE

MAP: 2 P54 **F2**

When you're done admiring Portofino's superyachts and designer shops, climb the steep path to **Castello Brown** *(castellobrown.com; tickets €12)*, the fourth incarnation of an early-medieval castle transformed by British diplomat Montague Yeats Brown into a private mansion in 1867. The grounds are exquisite, and the neo-Gothic rooms are filled with black-and-white photos of Portofino's erstwhile celebs. There's a reasonably priced (for Portofino) cafe on the terrace.

Fork Out for Italy's Poshest Beach

BEACH

MAP: 3 P54 **C4**

Spiaggia di Paraggi, 1km north of Portofino's harbour along the coast, is an exclusive but suitably gorgeous beach where a sun-lounger and umbrella will set you back a cool €200 at a private beach club. Alternatively, there's a tiny scoop of public beach or a narrow section of rocks accessible by a ladder from where you can launch into the turquoise water and watch both fish and Dior-wearing sunbathers. From Paraggi, a lovely seaside path threads north for 3km to the regal resort of Santa Margherita Ligure.

Green Dream

FARM TOURS

MAP: 4 P54 **B4**

Recent signs suggest Portofino might be shifting away from Gucci and Louis Vuitton and embracing more earthy pursuits. **La Portofinese** *(laportofinese.it)* is an agricultural project embracing self-sustainability and longstanding cultural traditions that offers various experiences in several locations around the village, including an eco-farm (producing honey, olives, vegetables and grapes), an osteria, a restored mill-museum, a terrace bar next to Portofino's lighthouse and a wine bar near the Piazzetta called Ü Caban (p69). Cooking classes and eco-farm visits headline the activities. Book online.

Founded in the mid-2010s by a local Portofinese, Mino Viacava, the company is family-run and heavily invested in organic farming, zero-kilometre food and renewable energy (solar panels, wind turbines and hydro-microturbines are all used).

Admire Villa Durazzo MANSION

MAP: 6 P54 **B3**

Santa Margherita Ligure is a sumptuous town. For proof head directly to the exquisitely turned-out **Villa Durazzo** *(villadurazzo.it; adult/child €5.50/3)* on a hill behind the harbour.

Built in the 1670s by the noble Durazzo family over a former castle complex that rested on ancient Roman remains, the five-storey mansion was radically remodelled in the 1820s when many of its present neoclassical elements were added. The lavish Italian gardens that overlook Santa Margherita's beach and harbour are filled with lemon trees, hydrangeas and camellia hedges, and sport an elongated sea-facing balustrade lined with life-sized classical statues. You can look around the house for a small fee, perusing grand pianos, weighty chandeliers and a wispy ceiling fresco of the Virgin Mary surrounded by cherub-like angels. It's a popular wedding venue.

The adjacent **Chiesa di San Giacomo di Corte**, with its classic cream baroque facade, has a surprisingly ornate interior set off by Corinthian columns and lavish gold leaf.

A cafe is open year-round and the terrace makes an enchanting setting for a drink.

WHY I LOVE PORTOFINO

Yes, it's expensive and, yes, it can get a little crowded, but, despite the €8 cappuccinos and unashamed piazza poseurs, I've always loved Portofino. I usually approach it on the rugged Passo di Baccio trail, a tricky traverse across a cliff-face that requires firm handholds and steely nerves. Descending into the village from this rugged mini-wilderness, I get an entirely different vision than the assembled crowds of super-yachters. By the time I reach the busy harbourside, with my shirt soaked in sweat and my fingernails full of dirt, I'm more than ready for a fresh pastry in **Caffè Excelsior** (MAP: 5 P54 **D2**) and a civilised glass of wine in **Winterose** (p69) – whatever the price.

Brendan Sainsbury
Lonely Planet writer

See Santa Margherita's 'Diffused' Museum WALK

Rather than offer a run-of-the-mill civic museum in one confined space, Santa Margherita touts what it calls a **Museo Diffuso di Mare**, with an assemblage of varied sights dotted around the city explaining its longstanding relationship with the sea.

To follow the itinerary, pick up a brochure from **IAT Information Office** (MAP: 7 P54 C3; *comune.santa-margherita-ligure.ge.it)* on the beachfront or download the **Vesepia App**. For seafront sights, walk west from the info centre into the public gardens, where you can admire statues of Christopher Columbus, city patron Santa Margherita (St Margaret), and 'Hero of the Two Worlds' Giuseppe Garibaldi, the Ligurian general who helped unify Italy in the 1860s. Further along the promenade, overlooking the harbour, you'll see a small 16th-century castle, a Middle Eastern–style fish market renovated in 2014, and an old hand-operated winch left over from Santa Margherita's shipbuilding days. The length of the promenade can be incorporated into an evening stroll or as part of a longer walk to Portofino.

Lungomare Vittorio Veneto, Rapallo
KURLIN_CAFE/SHUTTERSTOCK ©

OPERATION GINNY

In March 1944 during World War II, 15 American soldiers landed near Framura on the Riviera Levante with the intent of blowing up a coastal train tunnel and breaking a key communication line in German-occupied Italy. But, disoriented after their crossing from Corsica, the soldiers missed their target and landed in the wrong place. Unsure of their next move, they ended up seeking refuge in a barn close to the nearby village of Bonassola. The men, most of whom were Italian Americans, were quickly rounded up and, despite the assurances of the Geneva Convention, taken to Ameglia near La Spezia and summarily shot. The tunnel is now part of the Levanto–Framura bike path.

Parade along Rapallo's Lungomare PROMENADE

MAP: 8 P54 C3

Writers WB Yeats, Max Beerbohm and Ezra Pound all found inspiration in Rapallo, much of it probably garnered while walking on the **Lungomare Vittorio Veneto**, the town's seafront promenade. With its bright-blue changing cabins, palm-fringed beach and diminutive 16th-century castle rising directly from the sea, it lends the town a poetic and nostalgic air. The Lungomare is at its busiest on Thursdays, when the stalls of the **Mercato del Giovedì** (Thursday market) are spread along the waterfront.

Drop by Camogli's Fish Festival FOOD

Pretty **Camogli**, 25km east of Genoa, remains a working fishing hub – the town's name means 'house of wives', hailing from the days when the womenfolk did the grunt-work while the husbands were away at sea. Come the second weekend in May, the town celebrates its maritime heritage with the **Sagra del Pesce**. MAP: 9 P54 A2). A huge fish fry takes place with hundreds of the local catch cooked in 3m-wide pans along the waterfront (tuna and anchovies are favourites). The night before the festival, an effigy of the patron saint of fishermen, San Fortunato, is carried through town and two giant bonfires are ignited at midnight, both competing for size and magnificence.

Muse on Sestri Levante's Silent Bay BEACH QUARTER

The day-trip-worthy seaside town of Sestri Levante has enchanted countless generations of visitors, most notably the Danish writer Hans Christian Andersen (1805–75) who fell for the setting while renting a room here in 1833. Baia delle Favole (Bay of Fables) was later named in his honour. It sits back-to-back to the more curvaceous **Baia del Silenzio** (MAP: 10 P65 A1; Bay of Silence), a small but beautiful bay that lies hidden just behind the historic quarter (Sestri is sometimes described as the town of 'two seas'). Go early or late in the day to enjoy the seascape at its silent best. You'll find a diminutive sandy beach, a fisherman sculpture, narrow boats dotting the shoreline and fine views of colourful villas framed against the green slopes beyond.

On a steep rise behind the beach, the 17th-century **Chiesa di Santa Maria Immacolata** (MAP: 11 P65 **A1**) is known for its delightful *presepe* (nativity scene) complete with thunder and lightning, masticating cows, flickering fires and dozens of mechanised villagers.

Delve into Liguria's Past MUSEUM

MAP: 12 P65 **A1**

One of the Riviera's better history museums, Sestri Levanto's **Museo Archeologico e della Città** *(adult/child €5/3)*, usually shortened to Musel, deserves an hour of quiet contemplation.

Spread across the 3rd and 4th floors of the attractive Palazzo Fascie (built in 1904 but stylistically appearing much older), it delves into the region's past with interactive exhibitions and displays of archaeological finds, some of which were uncovered from underwater sites. The scope is quite broad, and features works from the Palaeolithic period, the Roman era and the Middle Ages.

Pride of place goes to the Cippo del Monte Ramaceto, a rare 2000-year-old Roman boundary stone found on a nearby mountain in 2015 that marked the limits of an imperial estate. A second stone was found in 2024.

Catch a Wave in Levanto SURFING

MAP: 13 P65 **B3**

Malibu, it isn't – but Levanto's superb beach is arguably Italy's finest surfing spot outside Sardinia. You'll see boarders year-round, but November to April is the best season. There are several good spots on the *spiaggia* (beach), headlined by Casino, opposite the town's erstwhile gambling joint, a long lefthander that forms on a shifting sandbar. **Brothers Surf House** (*brothersurf.com*; p69) in town rents boards and offers lessons.

Divert Along Levanto's Via Guani STREET

MAP: 14 P65 **B4**

Via Guani is a quiet lane, located a few blocks from the tumult of the beach, that winds its way past some of Levanto's oldest buildings and is worth a leisurely wander. Don't miss stately former noble residences like number 37, known as Palazzo delle Sirene, dating back to the 16th century. The street intersects with the Piazza del Popolo, where you'll find the 800-year-old loggia *medievale,* its columns hiding a small enclosure with the remains of a 13th-century fresco.

SESTRI LEVANTE TO LEVANTO

For more see
Experiences p60
Eating p67
Drinking p69
Shopping p69

Sestri Levante
12 Museo Archeologico e della Città
22
10 11 Baia del Silenzio
Chiesa di Santa Maria Immacolata
Casarza Ligure
A12
Moneglia
Ligurian Sea
Deiva Marina
Framura
17 27 Bonassola
See Levanto
0 5 km
0 2.5 miles

Levanto
Via Emanuele Zoppi
Via Jacopo da Levanto
24
Via Giuseppe Garibaldi
Passeggiata a Mare
Corso Italia
19
33
13 Brothers Surf House
Via Dante Alighieri
28
Via M Vinzoni
Via Guani
Piazza Staglieno
14 Via Guani
15 Sensafreni Bike Shop
Via Cantarana
Via Prealba
Ligurian Sea
0 100 m

Cycle path through railway tunnels
MARTI BUG CATCHER/SHUTTERSTOCK ©

Tunnel Along the Coast CYCLING
It takes effort to detach yourself from the spirit-lifting Italian atmosphere of beach-town Levanto, Liguria's surfing capital, but – with a free afternoon and a rentable pair of wheels – you can cruise along a smooth, flat bike path through a succession of old railway tunnels as far as Framura 6km to the northwest.

The first stop is the village of **Bonassola**, whose flower-lined streets and grey-sand beach are framed by forested hills and an abundance of seafood restaurants.

Another 3km along the path brings you to **Framura**, a commune of several disparate hamlets perched on a steep hillside.

The bike path ends at the railway station (where a real line appears). From here, you can walk down to an unadorned briny harbour. The final stretch of the ride is through a dark, dripping tunnel that American soldiers tried unsuccessfully to blow up during WWII (p63).

Several outfitters in Levanto rent out bikes, including **Sensafreni Bike Shop** (MAP: 15 P65 **B4**; *from €10 per day*) in Plaza del Populo.

Best Places for...

€ Budget €€ Midrange €€€ Top End

See p54 & p65 for map of locations

Eating

Seafood by the Sea

Hostaria Vecchia Rapallo €€
MAP: P54 16 C3
Aside from seafood dishes, this snug *hostaria* (traditional eating joint) tucked behind Rapallo's Lungomare serves Genovese- (pesto), farmer- (artichokes), street food- (fried fish cones) and truffle-themed menus. *12.30-2.30pm & 6-11pm*

Osteria Antica Guetta €€
MAP: P65 17 E4
Hire a bike in Levanto and cycle to lunch in nearby Bonassola where the Guetta serves outstanding seafood dishes from an elevated spot overlooking the beach. *noon-3pm & 7-10pm Thu-Tue*

Da Paolo €€
see Map P54 9 A2
Up a back lane from the waterfront, stylish Da Paolo has Camogli's best fish and seafood, all fresh off the boats and done in a variety of simple local styles. *noon-2.30pm & 7.30-10.30pm Wed-Sat, 7.30-10.50pm Sun*

Ola Blu €€
MAP: P54 18 C3
Right on the beach in San Michele di Pagana in Rapallo, the 'Blue Wave' offers traditional seafood (octopus, clams, prawns) in a bright modish interior that exudes a classy ambience. *10.30am-3pm & 6.30-10pm*

Antica Trattoria Centro €€
Map P65 19 A3
Classic Levanto trattoria, right down to the wood and wicker chairs and mostly Italian clientele. It conjures excellent tricks with seafood, especially the risotto. *12.30-2.30pm & 7.30-10pm Wed-Mon*

L'Altro Eden €€€
Map P54 20 C3
Santa Margherita's ultimate gourmet seafood spot is right on the harbour. Fish is served by weight, but they are best known for *crudo* (raw fish) and risotto with fresh prawns or squid ink. *7.30pm-midnight daily & 12.30-2.30pm Sat & Sun*

La Cantina €€€
Map P54 21 B4
Secluded spot in a cove in San Fruttuoso shaded by trees that's ideal for a lazy lunch based around prawns, clams and other bounty of the sea. *12.30-6pm*

Local Ligurian Food

Osteria Mattana €
Map P65 22 A1
A cellar-like two-room restaurant in Sestri Levante with hearty home-cooked dishes, a chalkboard menu, shared tables and outstanding prices. It's busy, friendly and exciting on the palate. *7.30-10.30pm*

Ö Bansin €€

Map P54 23 C2

Classic backstreet trattoria in Rapallo, in business since 1907, where comforting Ligurian classics are served with *molto amor* (much love). There's an airy garden courtyard to enjoy in summer. *noon-2pm & 7-10pm Tue-Sun*

Wine Art €€

see Map P54 18 C3

Tucked behind the cute beach of San Michele di Pagana between Santa Margherita and Rapallo, this restaurant-deli plates up superb *mandilli de sea* (lasagne-like pasta) doused in pesto. *7am-12am*

Ristorante Moresco €€

Map P65 24 B3

A chef-driven restaurant in Levanto that has a loyal local following for its superb seafood and pasta dishes served at reasonable prices. *7-9.45pm Tue-Fri, noon-2pm & 7-10pm Sat & Sun*

La Cucina di Nonna Nina €€

Map P54 25 A3

In the leafy heights of San Rocco di Camogli you'll find the only Slow Food–recommended restaurant along the coast, named for grandmother Nina, whose heirloom recipes have been handed down with love. *12.30-3pm & 7.30-10.30pm Thu-Tue*

Ristorante Puny €€€

Map P54 26 D1

Despite adhering to the standard Portofino business model (busy and expensive), Puny is one of the better places in the Piazzetta to recline with food that sticks loyally to Ligurian specialities, especially seafood. *12.30-2.30pm & 7.30-10.30pm Fri-Wed*

Cafes & Snacks

Caffè delle Rose €

Map P65 27 E4

The ultimate cycle- n-for-a-sandwich cafe in Bonassola, one block back from the beach, where you can digest your anchovies and artichokes under the trellises. *7am-11pm*

Revello €

see Map P54 9 A2

Join the queue in Camogli's favourite focaccia joint for a revered slice of their *focaccia di Recco* – a slightly flaky variety stuffed with stracchino cheese. There's no seating but the nearby harbour is a comfortable alternative. *8am-7.30pm*

Pasticceria Oneto €

see Map P54 7 C3

Busy, old-school pastry shop and cafe in Santa Margherita Ligure populated by locals who pop in for *panini*, *bruschette* and seasonal tarts, and linger with an espresso. *7am-8pm*

Pasticceria Bianchi €

Map P65 28 C3

An elegant historic cafe in Levanto where you can enjoy hot chocolate and croissants amid wood, tiles and polished glass. *7.30am-1pm & 4-7pm Tue-Sun*

Cafe Pasticceria Canepa 1862 €

see Map P54 23 C2

When all you want for breakfast is a cappuccino and a fresh pistachio brioche, head to Canepa in Rapallo, which has been knocking out sweet *colazioni* since Garibaldi's day. *6am-12.30pm & 3.30-7.30pm Tue-Sun*

Casa delle Tortore €€

see Map P54 6 B3

Foliage, fragrance, statues, sea views and coffee: there aren't many places as romantic as the gardens of Villa Durazzo in Santa Margherita to imbibe good caffeine. Spring and summer only. *11am-6pm Sat & Sun*

Perfect Pizza

Pizzeria La Cava al Mare €€

see Map P54 18 C3

In case you thought the Golfo di Tigullio was too posh for pizza, head over to Rapallo where this unfancy, tourist-free place knocks out classic pies with bubbled, burnt crusts. *noon-2pm & 7-11pm Tue-Sun*

Pizzeria El Portico €€

Map P54 29 D2

Wander a block from Portofino's extortionate harbour and pizzas can be had here for under €10. There's also octopus salad, *vongole* (clams) and Genovese favourites on the wonderfully unpretentious chequered tablecloths. *noon-3.30pm & 5.30-11.30pm Wed-Mon*

Drinking

Wine & Cocktails

Ü Caban

Map P54 30 D2

Ingeniously crafted wine bar on Portofino's Piazzetta whose interior has been fashioned like a boat. 'On board' you can sample food and wine from the owner's local farm. *noon-11pm Wed-Mon*

Al Faro di Portofino

Map P54 31 C4

Portofino's slightly out of the way 'lounge bar' has a small outdoor terrace nestled beneath the spectacularly sited lighthouse. By Portofino standards, it's decidedly rustic, but the cocktails are creative. *10.30am-10pm*

Sabot Italia

see Map P54 7 C3

Sink into a sofa or grab a street-side table on Santa Margherita's seafront and enjoy well-made cocktails, upbeat jazzy grooves and friendly banter with the staff. *4.30pm-3am*

Winterose

Map P54 32 E1

This Yachties' favourite is a wine shop with an affiliated bar that offers good deals on charcuterie boards and glasses of *vino*. It offers Portofino sophistication without the unnecessary pretension. *11am-8pm Thu-Tue*

Bars Near the Beach

La Mancina

see Map P54 9 A2

A couple of stools outside will give you a sea view, but the real action at this Camogli boozer is inside, where dog-eared books line the walls and locals chat with the owner over *spritz* or beer. *6.30pm-2am*

Contro Vento

Map P65 33 A3

A drinking and grazing bar a block from Levanto's beach where patrons perch at alfresco tables enjoying Franziskaner and Leffe on draft, good wines by the glass and first-rate cocktails. *11am-2am*

Shopping

Sport

Brothers Surf House

see Map P65 15 B4

As well as renting boards and offering surf lessons, this cool Levanto surf store sells a full range of branded gear and clothing, both trendy and practical. It also covers skateboarding. *10am-1pm & 3.30-7.30pm*

Art

Galleria d'Arte Portofino

Map P54 34 D2

One of Portofino's best 'just looking not buying' stores (unless you're suitably loaded), this family-run gallery in the Piazzetta displays an ever-changing assemblage of contemporary works, many depicting local scenes. *10am-8pm*

Hike the Alta Via delle Cinque Terre

The AV5T trail is a 35km-long path that threads its way along cliffs and ridgetops between Porto Venere and Levanto avoiding entering the Cinque Terre towns themselves. In contrast to the uber-popular Green-Blue trail (SVA) that is rarely out of sight of the sea, the AV5T is more secluded and wooded – and notably less crowded.

START	END	LENGTH
Porto Venere	Levanto	35km; 8–10 hours

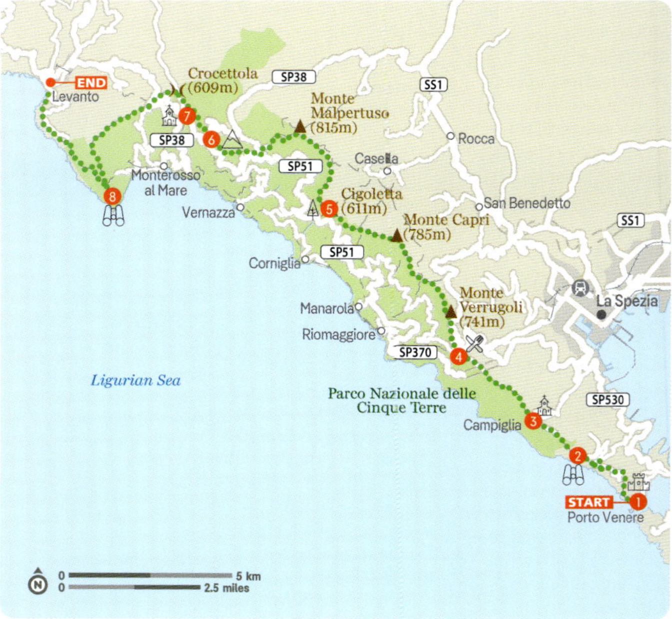

1 Spectacular Start

The initial climb out of **Porto Venere**, past the terraced Doria Castle, is steep and dramatic, skirting towering cliffs revered by rock-climbers. Enjoy views back over the haunting Chiesa di San Pietro before the path dissolves into woodland around the back of Monte Muzzerone, a sheer cliff topped by a 19th-century fort.

2 Close to the Edge

After a short stretch on a rural lane, the AV5T switches back towards the coast at Sella Derbi where the narrow trail teeters spine-tinglingly close to the cliff-edge. An observation point called **Pitone** captures the drama.

3 Village Stop

The ruins of a 17th-century windmill welcome you to the small settlement of **Campiglia**. Walk past the village church and drop into the local shop if you're feeling hungry already.

4 Mid-Trail Nexus

Named for the telegraph wires that used to be strung here, **Colle del Telegrafo** is a popular trail crossroads and home to the best restaurant on the AV5T. You can refuel with plates of *bruschette* and cold drinks, while resting on the terrace overlooking the sea.

5 Into the Woods

The AV5T now enters a long wooded section with the sea glimmering like a blue suggestion through the thick foliage. Mountain biking is popular on the 7km stretch to **Cigoletta** (elevation 611m), while hikers are scarce.

6 Hitting the Peak

Il Termine is an open clearing roughly 7km from Cigoletta. There are some gentle uphill climbs on this stretch as you pass along the slopes of Mt Malpertuso, the highest point of Cinque Terre at 815m.

7 Pilgrim's Pause

After Il Termine, the route cuts down a road to Monterosso's **Santuario Madonna di Soviore** (worth an elongated rest-stop) and then follows trail 591 to a road crossing at Colle di Gritta.

8 The Final Push

Trail 591 passes through scattered pines, Mediterranean scrub and forests of holm oaks to the jutting **Punta Mesco** peninsula where you can see all five Cinque Terre villages in one sweeping vista. The ruins of an old hermitage dedicated to St Anthony lie at the end of a short spur off the main trail. It's a further 4km along the coast to the finish at Levanto.

See p83
for eating, drinking and shopping listings

Explore
Monterosso al Mare

The most accessible village by car and the only Cinque Terre settlement to sport a proper stretch of beach, Monterosso is the least quintessential of the quintet. Indeed, in 1948 it was briefly excluded from the famous five. The westernmost village is known for its lemon trees and anchovies, both of which turn up on plates in local restaurants. There's also an under-appreciated wine culture and an abundance of well-stocked *enoteche* (wine bars) for tastings. Split in two by the blustery San Cristoforo promontory, Monterosso's new and old halves are linked by an underground tunnel. Fegina, to the west, is a beach strip not unlike neighbouring Levanto. The labyrinthine old quarter is similar in size and atmosphere to its four siblings to the east.

Getting Around

Walking

Despite being Cinque Terre's most spread-out village, Monterosso is easily walkable. A short tunnel connects the old and new sections under the San Cristoforo promontory.

Bus

There's a twice-daily bus from Monterosso up to the Santuario della Madonna di Soviore.

Car

Monterosso is the only Cinque Terre village with parking close to the centre. Fegina Beach has a car park with 300 spaces a five-minute walk from the train station.

Monterosso al Mare

TRABANTOS/SHUTTERSTOCK ©

THE BEST

FOCACCIA
Il Massimo della Focaccia (p83)

HIKE WITH A VIEW
Punta Mesco (p81)

GLASS OF WINE
Enoteca Internazionale (p81)

GOURMET FOOD
Miky (p83)

PAINTING
Crucifixion by Van Dyck (allegedly; p77)

Walk Monterosso

This easy-to-navigate village amble incorporates both sides of Monterosso's personality, starting on its classic Riviera-style beach and concluding in its tightly coiled old-town streets, so typical of Cinque Terre. The views along the coast are expansive, dominated by the pine-dotted ridgetop of the Punta Mesco. Save time for some wine and anchovies afterwards.

START	END	LENGTH
Statua del Gigante	Via Roma	2.2km; two hours

0 200 m
0 0.1 miles
SP38
END
6
Via Roma
5
Piazza Minzoni
4
Monterosso
2
Via Fegina
3
Salita dei Cappuccini
1
START
Ligurian Sea

1 Injured Neptune

Start your walk at the western (newer) end of Monterosso. On a small cliff fringing the beach stand the remains of a 14m-high giant Neptune, **Statua del Gigante**, built in 1910 to hold up the seaward edge of the Villa Palatine. The god of the sea suffered significant damages from Allied bombing in World War II.

2 Parading the Promenade

Walking eastward, you'll soon reach the promenade above the sea. Here you'll have a fine view over pebbly **Spiaggia di Fegina**, which fills up with sunbathers during the summer. Terrace cafes offer strategic spots to take in the scene.

3 WWII Defences

Instead of entering the tunnel beneath the San Cristoforo promontory, take the path leading up to the right. You'll soon reach stairs tumbling down to a restaurant, and just beyond an old **pillbox** built by the Germans to repel an Allied invasion during World War II. It stands as an ugly anachronism to a less peaceful era.

4 A Calmer Beach

The smaller of Monterosso's two beaches, **Spiaggia Tragagia**, lies to the east of the San Cristoforo promontory. It's backed by a series of railway arches, which act as a gateway to the old town. The sand is gravelly here while the sea is relatively calm, protected by a breakwater and harbour wall. There are free access areas and several private beach clubs.

5 Glories of Gothic

Continue into the village and stop by a splendid old-town treasure, the striped **Chiesa San Giovanni Battista**. This Gothic church dates from the early 14th century and has a few notable works within, including a painting of the Madonna del Rosario, attributed to the school of Luca Cambiaso.

6 Shopping Street

End your wander in the heart of old Monterosso on the animated **Via Roma**. This street is lined with shops, restaurants, bakeries and wine bars. Treat yourself to a glass of Cinque Terre's finest at the Enoteca Internazionale (p81). The terrace is well placed for watching village life unfold.

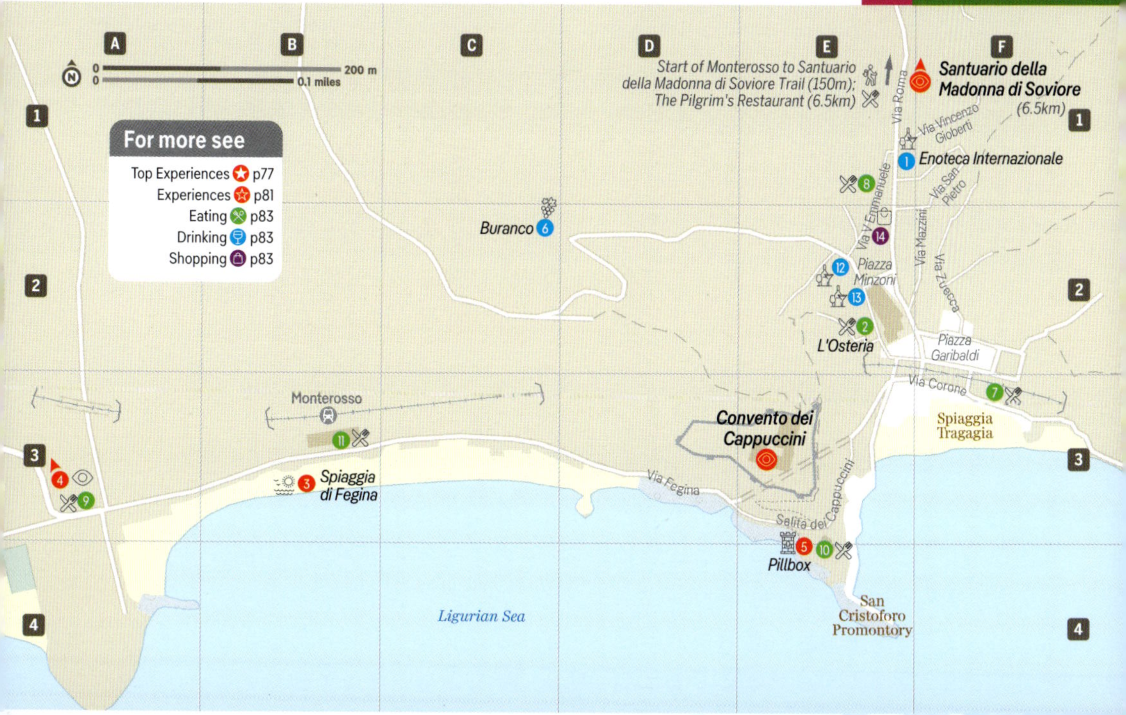

A
B
C
D
E
F
1
2
3
4
0 200 m
0 0.1 miles
For more see
Top Experiences p77
Experiences p81
Eating p83
Drinking p83
Shopping p83
Start of Monterosso to Santuario della Madonna di Soviore Trail (150m); The Pilgrim's Restaurant (6.5km)
Santuario della Madonna di Soviore (6.5km)
Via Roma
Via Vincenzo Gioberti
1 Enoteca Internazionale
8
Via San Pietro
Via V Emmanuele
14
Via Mazzini
Via Zuecca
Buranco 6
12
Piazza Minzoni
13
2 L'Osteria
Piazza Garibaldi
Via Corone
7
Spiaggia Tragagia
Monterosso
11
Convento dei Cappuccini
4
9
3 Spiaggia di Fegina
Via Fegina
Salita dei Cappuccini
5
10
Pillbox
San Cristoforo Promontory
Ligurian Sea

★ TOP EXPERIENCE

Convento dei Cappuccini

On a promontory high above Monterosso, the still-functioning Convent of Capuchin Friars has been around for over 400 years and remains a much-loved part of village life. The short but steep climb to its ecclesial core offers stirring coastal views and the chance to glean an understanding of the strict Franciscan religious order.

MAP P76 **E3**

The Convent and its Friars

The convent was built between 1618 and 1622 for Capuchin friars who hailed from a religious order that had been founded in 1525. Capuchins sought to re-embrace the strict discipline and austere lifestyle first advocated by St Francis of Assisi (1181–1226). They were famed for their long, hooded habits and skill as vegetable farmers.

Changing laws meant the convent was shuttered twice during the 19th century. Since reopening, it has been in continuous operation since 1895.

Chiesa di San Francesco

From a distance, the facade of the convent's church seems to be made of marble when, in fact, it's a fine trompe l'oeil (stucco painted in black-and-white stripes). Inside, one of the great treasures of the monastery hangs on the left side of the church. *Crucifixion*, flanked by two exquisitely painted figures, is a masterpiece long attributed to Flemish painter Van Dyck, although modern experts are more sceptical. Notwithstanding, it's a beautiful work. An electronic panel below explains both the intricacies of the painting and the unique architecture of the church.

PLANNING TIP
You can reach the convent from the centre of old Monterosso. You can also get there coming directly from the train station – just take the seaside path, rather than entering the tunnel.

Scan for information on booking guided tours of the convent.

TRABANTOS/SHUTTERSTOCK ©

QUICK BREAK
If coming directly from the new part of town, stop first at the super-casual **Massimo della Focaccia**, which dispenses take-out focaccia slices and other snacks.

Cemetery

Keep walking uphill from the church and you'll soon reach the village cemetery. This was once where an 11th-century castle stood, surrounded by stout walls to protect against pirate attacks. Today, the ground amid the crumbling walls serves as the final resting place for villagers and parish priests. Some fine monuments stretch toward the sky and, if you wind your way up through the cemetery, you'll reach another panoramic lookout.

St Francis & the Wolf

On the walk up to the convent, a bronze sculpture of St Francis and his lupine friend sits on a gorgeous lookout over the seaside. With outstretched arm and paw, the pair indicate a stretch of mountain-backed coastline, with each of the tiny Cinque Terre villages visible from here.

★ TOP EXPERIENCE

Santuario della Madonna di Soviore

The largest and oldest of Cinque Terre's five medieval sanctuaries, the Santuario della Madonna di Soviore is a tranquil religious complex perched 470m above Monterosso amid holm oaks and cypress trees. Located at an important trail crossroads, it offers restaurant food and monastic rooms in a simple guesthouse.

MAP P76 **F1**

The Pietà Myth

Parts of the sanctuary's present structure date from the 11th century and a pilgrimage site has existed here since at least the 8th century. Imbued in medieval myth, the venerated wooden statue of Pietà (Mary cradling the dead body of Jesus) displayed in the church is of 15th-century provenance. The original statue was supposedly dug up by a priest in 740 who had been directed to the site by a white dove. The exact spot is marked by a small hexagonal chapel just below the sanctuary known as the Cappella del Ritrovamento.

PLANNING TIP

The sanctuary is the western terminus of the Strada dei Santuari, a 22km path that connects all five village sanctuaries. It takes around seven hours to complete.

The Church & its Development

The sanctuary itself inhabits an impressive terrace lined by majestic oak trees over 100 years old. The trees don't block the views which stretch as far as Corsica on a clear day.

Added to over the years, the sanctuary's most recent overhaul was in 2000. The single nave church has a richly frescoed ceiling, ornate chandeliers and a chessboard floor. The impressive Tuscan-made Agati organ hails from 1822 and is still used for concerts. Outside, the facade is embellished by a Gothic rose window and a

Scan for information about the restaurant, guesthouse and surrounding activities.

SASHA64F/SHUTTERSTOCK ©

QUICK BREAK
The sanctuary has its own eating establishment, **The Pilgrim's Restaurant**, selling snacks, drinks and fixed-price dinner menus for €20.

Romanesque bell tower with a muted spire. The large porticoed building next door is a guesthouse added in the 1700s. It remains in use today and is particularly popular with scouting groups.

Pilgrim's Path

To reach the sanctuary on foot, take trail 509 – the original pilgrim's route – from Monterosso's Via Roma. The ancient mule path leads up through olive and lemon trees and mixed forest, crossing a couple of roads. An iron cross and the mildewed Cappella del Ritrovamento set a palpable religious tone. The distance from Monterosso is 2.5km and takes around 1¾ hours.

The sanctuary also acts as an important way-station on the 35km Portovenere–Levanto trek, intersecting with path 591 that links Il Termine on the AV5T with Punta Mesco (pictured). If you don't fancy walking, the church is accessible via a couple of daily buses from Monterosso.

EXPERIENCES

Follow the Wine & Anchovies Trail

FOOD & WINE

To get a fully rounded taste of Monterosso, reserve time to sample two of its prized home-produced delicacies: wine and anchovies. The prime fishing season for anchovies is June and July, and, afterwards, anchovies are preserved in salt barrels to allow for year-round consumption.

The fish goes well with the dry, white Cinque Terre DOC wine. Monterosso has several cellar-like *enoteche* where you can savour this duo, not least **Enoteca Internazionale** (MAP: 1 P76 **E1**) where plates of anchovies come seasoned with a little olive oil and garlic.

Numerous other restaurants around town serve the wine-fish pairing in a variety of guises, including **L'Osteria** (MAP: 2 P76 **E2**), Miky (p83) and Trattoria da Oscar (p83).

Book Beach Time on Spiaggia di Fegina

BEACH

MAP: 3 P76 **B3**

For a day of sloth, head to the gravelly-sand expanses of **Spiaggia di Fegina** on the west side of the San Cristoforo promontory, Cinque Terre's only bona fide beach that's backed by an attractive promenade and lined with typical Italian *stabilimenti balneari* (private beach clubs). You'll pay around €20 a day for a sun-lounger and umbrella here. Alternatively, you can unfurl your towel on a much sought-after slither of *spiaggia libero* (free beach) at various points along the shore. The sea is clear and relatively warm by July. Bank on plenty of sun-bathing company.

Follow the Path to Punta Mesco

HIKE

MAP: 4 P76 **A3**

While most people hike east out of Monterosso on the famous Sentiero Verde-Azzurro (SVA), it's worth heading west on trail 590 (technically an extension of the SVA) to the tall pine-speckled promontory known as **Punta Mesco**.

The 2km trail starts near the Statua del Gigante and ascends via steps and rough paths through pines, holm oaks and Mediterranean scrub, with the views becoming more majestic at each curve in the route. At panoramic Punta Mesco, the ruins of a small hermitage dedicated to St Anthony lie at the end of a short spur trail. The site dates from the 1300s and was gradually abandoned over the centuries. The brothers here kept an eye out for pirate ships on the horizon and lit signal fires to warn nearby villages of approaching corsairs. A newer *semaforo* (light station), also abandoned, sits nearby.

From the hermitage, you can carry on via path 591 to Levanto or track along the spine of the

MONTEROSSO'S FOOD FESTIVALS

The Sagra del Limone
At the end of May, the whole of Monterosso celebrates its lemons – which find their way into the cakes, juices and marmalades that you can sample at street stalls throughout the village.

Sagra dell'Acciuga Fritta e Sagra dell'Acciuga Salata
Monterosso has two events dedicated to anchovies. The Sagra dell'Acciuga Fritta is in June, celebrating freshly fished and fried anchovies, while the Sagra dell'Acciuga Salata is in September, starring salted anchovies ready to be stored away during the cold months.

promontory to Il Termine and the Santuario della Madonna di Soviore (p79).

Explore the San Cristoforo Promontory VIEWS

The prominent headland that demarcates Monterosso's old and new towns has long acted as an important defensive bastion. Rather than rushing through the tunnel between beaches, it's worth exploring the promontory's paved paths for vestiges of past fortifications built between the 11th and 20th centuries.

The hill's oldest surviving castle is incorporated into the town cemetery and encircled by the boundaries of the Capuchin convent at the promontory's highest point. Lower down, a rectangular 16th-century tower has been converted into a seafood restaurant called **Torre Aurora** (p83; *torreauroracinqueterre.com*). Visible below and reachable via stairs is a World War II **pillbox** (MAP: 5 P76 E3; p75).

The Agriturismo Experience FARM & WINE-TASTING

MAP: 6 P76 C2

A short 300m walk from Monterosso's Via Roma but belonging well and truly in the countryside, **Buranco** (*burancocinqueterre.it*) is an *agriturismo* (farm-stay accommodation), restaurant and wine-tasting experience. A verdant oasis of terraced vineyards, lemon trees and rolling lawns, it produces classic DOC Cinque Terre white wines as well as grappa, *limoncino* (the Italian Riviera's answer to the Amalfi Coast's lemon-flavored *limoncello*) and the local dessert wine that's even harder to produce than it is to pronounce: Sciacchetrà (*shah-keh-trah*).

Before or after a tasting on the verandah, you can wander the vineyards to get a sense of the challenges of working the steeply terraced hillsides. Buranco also rents out several simple apartments on the property, some with terraces overlooking the vineyards.

See p76 for map of locations

Best Places for...

€ Budget €€ Midrange €€€ Top End

Eating

Flavours of the Sea

Ristorante Belvedere €€
7 F3
With tables overlooking the beach, this unpretentious restaurant is known for its house special, the amphora Belvedere, (lobster, mussel, swordfish, octopus and clam stewed in traditional earthenware). *noon-2.30pm & 7-9.30pm Wed-Mon*

Trattoria da Oscar €€
 E1
Tiny, family-run joint in Monterosso's historic centre with outstanding anchovies, *vongole* (clams) and gnocchi dishes. *noon-2.30pm & 7-9.30pm Sat-Thu*

Miky €€€
 A3
As posh as restaurants get in Cinque Terre, Miky is a gourmand's favourite with Michelin credentials, that serves fish-filled tasting menus. *noon-2.30pm & 7-11pm Wed-Mon*

Torre Aurora €€€
 E4
Set in a 13th-century tower with a terrace overlooking the sea, the seafood goes down well with the sweeping views. *noon-10.30pm*

Street Food

Il Massimo della Focaccia €
 B3
Walk-up bakery on the beachfront with the best crispy focaccia in Cinque Terre. Join the queue for a range of oven-fresh flatbreads including pesto. *9am-6pm Thu-Tue*

Drinking

Local Wine

Enoteca Internazionale
see  E1
With over 500 varieties, Monterosso evinces one of the best places in Cinque Terre to discover regional wines. Pair the booze with local food on the front terrace in Via Roma. *8am-11pm*

Enoteca da Eliseo
 E2
Going strong since the 1980s, this back-lane *enoteca* has outdoor tables and a selection of wines and grappas. *2-11pm Wed-Mon*

La Cantina del Pescatore
 E2
A purveyor of local wines served with superb pesto-topped *bruschetta*, the Pescatore also sells Cinque Terre–made sauces, honey and olive oils. *8am-9pm Mon-Sat*

Shopping

Creative Ceramics

Fabbrica d'Arte Monterosso
14 E2
Several generations of one family create and sell the upscale ceramics on display at this shop with vases, bowls, jugs, platters and decorative tiles all featuring elegant designs. *10am-7pm*

WALKING TOUR

Sentiero Verde-Azzurro

The 12km-long Sentiero Verde-Azzurro (SVA) trail is an ancient cliffside path that links all five Cinque Terre villages in a spectacular traverse. Its historical significance, unique farming terraces and unfailing good looks mean it's mega-popular and one of the few trails in Italy you must pay to use.

PLANNING TIP
Due to its enduring popularity, a payment system has been installed to control trail usage. Walkers must purchase a **Cinque Terre Trekking Card** (adult/child €7.50/4.50) before setting out.

Overview of the Path

The SVA is split into four sections. The segments between Monterosso al Mare, Vernazza and Corniglia traverse ancient stone terraces and skillfully tilled agricultural plots. They measure 3.5km and 3.8km respectively. There are control booths at either end where wardens take payments and check passes.

The 2.2km section between Manarola and Corniglia has been closed since 2013. A higher, steeper path via Volastra is offered as an alternative.

The section between Riomaggiore and Manarola, known as the Via dell'Amore, is the shortest and easiest.

The walk takes up to six hours in its entirety. Many people spread it over two days. There is currently no charge to walk the Corniglia–Manorola portion.

Scan for information on how to buy the Cinque Terre Trekking Card.

Monterosso al Mare to Vernazza

The ascent out of Monterosso begins gently, passing vineyards with periodic lookouts back to the seaside village. Soon, the climbing begins in earnest as you tackle many flights of steps (there are over 500 throughout the walk). Native Bosco, Albarola and Vermentino grapes are cultivated in the region to create classic varieties of Cinque

PHOTOCREO MICHAL BEDNAREK/SHUTTERSTOCK ©

Terre DOC white wine. Aside from vines, you'll also see lemons, artichokes, capers and herbs – all produced sustainably.

As the path continues uphill, the landscape leaves the coast behind and winds its way inland. You'll pass moss-covered stone walls, thick blooms of wisteria and trickling streams crisscrossing the path – with the occasional stone bridge. Inland views reveal a fertile valley with a patchwork of farms hemmed in by rolling green hills rising behind. Slow down to admire the olive trees and figs, strands of wildflowers and the odd cactus.

Three-quarters of the way to Vernazza the path veers back towards the coast. The landscape here is wild and untouched with distant views of steep mountainsides intersected with the foaming waters of the wave-battered shore.

QUICK BREAK

Perched on the terraces in Prevo between Corniglia and Vernazza, with outdoor tables offering magnificent views, the rural **Il Gabbiano** services hikers with cold drinks, *panini* and other snacks.

TWO TYPES OF CARD
Opt for the **Cinque Terre Trekking Card** if you just want to hike on the SVA between the villages, and the **Treno MS Card** if you want to include unlimited train travel.

Vernazza to Corniglia

Stairs out of Vernazza lead up to a lookout from where the village appears small and fragile against the tempestuous sea. Beyond, uneven stone steps zigzag past olive trees, bushy forest and long-abandoned terraced gardens.

The path is compacted dirt or flat stones in places, with plenty of steps throughout. Along the cliffs, wooden railings provide added protection, although the trail suffers significant wear and tear during the rainy months. Soon, you'll reach a wilder part of the coast with views of densely forested slopes blanketed with Mediterranean vegetation stretching ahead, and the cliffs to your right thick with Indian fig opuntia and agave plants.

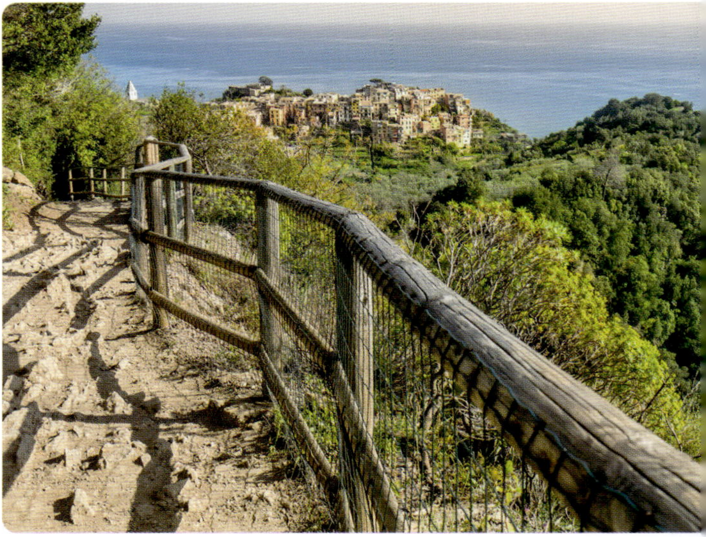

Around midway between Vernazza and Corniglia, you'll pass the hamlet of **Prevo**. The tiny settlement was founded in the 16th century by families of mountain shepherds who migrated here. Protected by dry stone walls, the terraces nurture vegetable gardens, lemon and pomegranate trees, as well as cherries and quince. Corniglia is around 1.5km further east (pictured).

The Missing Link

The section of the SVA between Corniglia and Manarola, sometimes referred to as trail 592-2, has been closed since 2013 due to landslides after heavy rains. This relatively flat 2.2km segment runs close to the shoreline from Corniglia's seaside train station to the Punta Bonfiglio in Manarola. As an alternative, walkers are directed higher up the hillside on paths 506, 586 and 587, respectively, to reach Corniglia via the hamlet of Volastra.

Via dell'Amore

The 1km-long section of the SVA between Manarola and Riomaggiore is Cinque Terre's most popular trail. It was originally built in the 1920s to link two erstwhile service roads leftover from the construction of the regional railway line. Grafted into the cliffside, the path took 11 years to complete and helped bring together the populations of the two geographically divided villages. The name 'the path of love' is a nod to the number of intervillage marriages the opening of the path engendered.

Unstable land is a perennial problem in the area, and things came to a head in 2012 when four Australian tourists were injured in a rockslide. The trail was closed and remained in limbo for over a decade, bogged down by bureaucracy and additional damage from rough seas. It eventually reopened in 2024 after an estimated €22 million of repairs. To control tourist numbers, entry is by guided tour only. Slots can be booked online for 30-minute multilingual tours that leave on the half-hour.

TRAIL NUMBERING

Formerly known as Trail No 2 or the Sentiero Azzurro (blue path), Cinque Terre's arterial path is now usually labelled SVA (Sentiero Verde-Azzurro) on maps and signposts, or sometimes Trail 592.

See p96
for eating,
drinking and
shopping
listings

Explore Vernazza

Wrapped around a splendid natural harbour, Vernazza, along with Riomaggiore, is imbued with a genuine fishing village ambience. Unlike the other Cinque Terre villages, its medieval church abuts the water, and its ruined Doria Castle, which is perched atop a rocky knoll above town, is open to visitors (although there's little to see apart from the views). The harbour is the epicentre of the village and its best open-air amusement spot, with a tiny sandy beach, a sheltered bay that's safe for swimming and a potpourri of restaurants where you can linger over the day's fresh catch with a glass of prosecco.

Getting Around

Walking

Vernazza's train station is a short walk from the harbour. The Sentiero Verde-Azzurro (SVA, p84) passes directly through town heading east to Corniglia and west to Monterosso al Mare. The streets on either side of arterial Via Roma are steep with many steps.

Bus

There are three local buses a day from the village to the Santuario della Madonna di Reggio.

Car

Driving in the village is for residents only. The closest you can get by car is a parking lot 1km to the east on SP-51.

Vernazza
SIMON DANNHAUER/SHUTTERSTOCK ©

THE BEST

STREET FOOD
Batti Batti (p95)

CROWD ESCAPE
Santuario della Madonna di Reggio (p95)

VIEWPOINT
Doria Castle (p91)

GELATO FIX
Il Porticciolo (p95)

SEAFOOD DINING EXPERIENCE
Belforte (p96)

WALKING TOUR

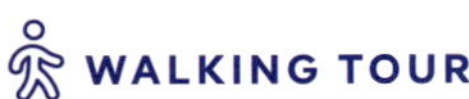

Walk Vernazza

Vernazza isn't large but you'll need to zigzag around a bit to capture the best spots. Expect plenty of company on this stroll, particularly in narrow Via Visconti at the seaside end of Via Roma, a major congestion point at peak hours. To beat the day-tripping crowds, go early in the morning or late in the afternoon.

START	END	LENGTH
Vernazza train station	Via Vernazza	1.5km; 1½ hours

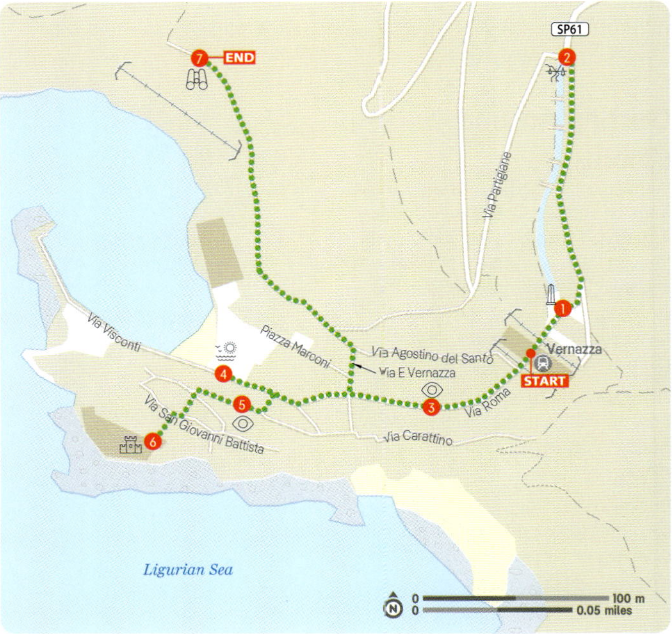

1 War Memorial

Just uphill from the train station, the tiny **Piazzetta dei Caduti** gathers a mix of young families and old-timers seeking a reprieve from the busyness down by the harbour. In one corner of the plaza is a monument dedicated to victims of the world wars, with names inscribed on a marble plaque.

2 Local Stream

Keep strolling uphill along Via Roma and you'll soon find yourself beside the gently flowing **Torrente Vernazzola**. This stream was once much wider and was a gathering spot for locals who did their washing on the riverbank. Today, it's fringed by modern apartment blocks, with several tiny bridges over the stream.

3 Village Artery

Catch your breath then make the descent into the heart of Vernazza along **Via Roma**. This gently winding lane is packed with shops, restaurants and cafes. Just past the train station, a poster on the left wall shows the devastation wrought by floods in October 2011 (p95). There's also a small stone chapel further along dedicated to Santa Marta.

4 Beach & Harbour

At the end of Via Roma, you'll get funnelled into open **Piazza Marconi** flanked by restaurants, with outdoor tables sitting pretty just above the water's edge.

5 Back Streets

Double back and turn right into **Via Guidoni** for a glimpse of an age-old community of tightly packed dwellings cascading the hillsides with window-box flowers and lines of laundry flapping in the breeze.

6 Battlements

Arranged around a 70m-high spur, Vernazza's **Doria Castle** dates from around 1000 but is today largely a ruin except for the circular tower in the centre of the esplanade. The castle changed hands between Pisa and Genoa in medieval times and during World War II was used as an anti-aircraft post by the German army.

7 Lofty Lookout

Descend back to Via Roma and continue up the stairs on the opposite side. Keep following this path and you'll reach a **lookout** above the church, offering a handsome view over the harbour and the terraced vineyards just out of town.

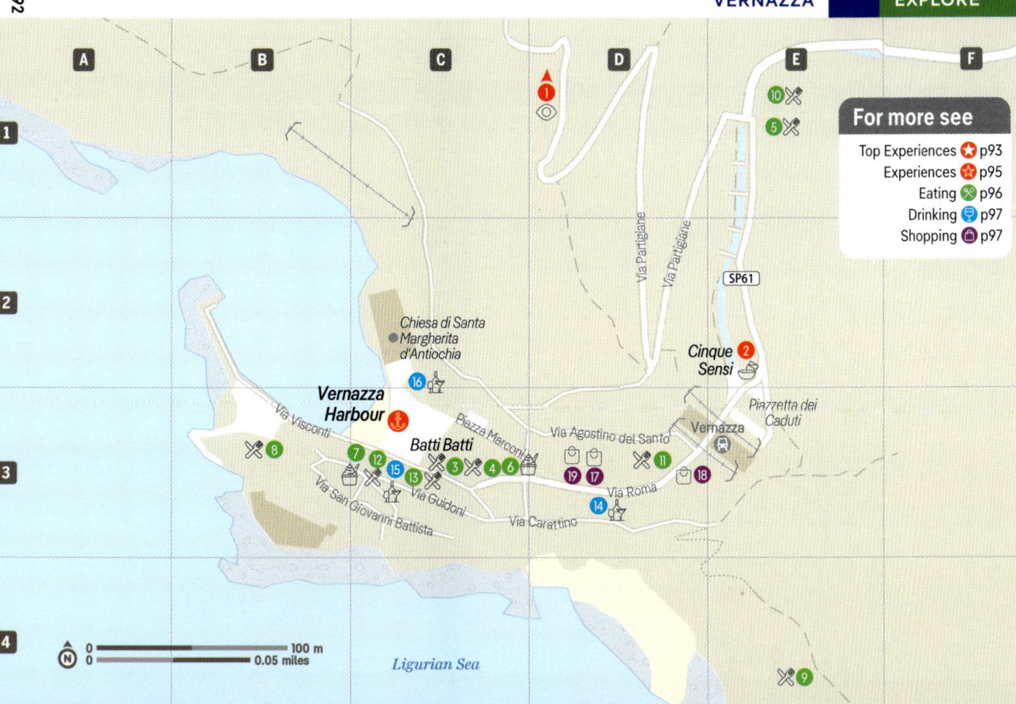
For more see
Top Experiences p93
Experiences p95
Eating p96
Drinking p97
Shopping p97
Chiesa di Santa Margherita d'Antiochia
Vernazza Harbour
Batti Batti
Cinque Sensi
Piazzetta dei Caduti
Vernazza
SP61
Via Partigiane
Via Partigiane
Via Visconti
Piazza Marconi
Via Agostino del Santo
Via Roma
Via Guidoni
Via San Giovanni Battista
Via Carattino
Ligurian Sea
0 100 m
0 0.05 miles

★ TOP EXPERIENCE

Vernazza Harbour

Of all the Cinque Terre harbours, Vernazza's is the largest and most action-packed with its main square sitting flush against the water. This is where most enamoured visitors come to savour their take-outs, wrestle for elbow room on a tiny beach and brave the clear but often chilly water.

MAP P92 **C3**

Piazza Marconi

Village life and tourist gatherings coexist around this gorgeous waterfront square. On clear days, the terrace restaurants and cafes, whose tables fill the piazza, provide a magnificent setting for a fresh seafood meal or an afternoon cocktail. You'll also find some of Vernazza's best gelato here (take a bow, Il Porticciolo; p96), which you can take away to enjoy on a seawall that protrudes into the harbour. When the tourists go home in the winter, the tables disappear and fishers pull their boats up onto the pavestones.

PLANNING TIP
Book an alfresco restaurant table for sunset. It's a magical time to be out facing the water. Recommended spots are **Ananasso Bar** (p97) and **Gianni Franzi** (p97).

The Nanoscopic Beach

On warm summer days, the tiny parcel of sand abutting the piazza draws sunbathers to the water's edge (arrive early for your own square metre). Normally the waters are fairly calm here, with boats bobbing just offshore and children splashing about in the cool sea. You can also rent boats (kayaks, motorboats) and arrange water-based excursions.

Swimming & Lounging

If the beach is too crowded, follow the narrow harbourside lane past the church where you can lounge on the flat rocks at the water's edge or float idly while trains glide past above the high stone

Scan for information on Cinque Terre and Vernazza.

LILIANA MARMELO/SHUTTERSTOCK ©

QUICK BREAK
The best spot for snack food (focaccia), coffee and cocktails on the square is **Ananasso Bar** (p97) in the shadow of the church.

wall fringing the lapping waves. Another popular swimming spot is from a smaller piazza in front of the Belforte restaurant (p96) to the west of the harbour wall.

Chiesa di Santa Margherita d'Antiochia

The waterfront is dominated by this compact Ligurian-Gothic **church** (pictured), built on a small seafront promontory in 1318 on the site of an 11th-century Romanesque building. According to legend, the church was constructed after a box containing the bones of St Margaret washed up on a nearby beach. It is notable for its unusual 40m-tall octagonal tower topped with a dome.

Inside, the church is relatively austere although it contains several 17th-century paintings and a wooden crucifix attributed to Anton Maria Maragliano. The views through the narrow arched windows of the unruly sea framed by harbour boats and headlands are outstanding.

EXPERIENCES

Pilgrimage to the Reggio Sanctuary

HIKE & CHURCH

MAP: 1 P92 **D1**

This climb to an emblematic sanctuary, on an ancient overgrown trail lined by corroded stations of the cross, is bliss. The **Santuario della Madonna di Reggio** is a solitary church guarded by an avenue of trees including an 800-year-old cypress. The Romanesque facade dates from the 13th century and contains a venerated 14th-century painting of the Black Madonna and child.

A terracotta-red 'guesthouse' was built onto the back of the church in the 1800s but now stands mostly idle. Amid the surrounding trees, you'll spot several mildewed statues and a small grotto. The path to the sanctuary begins 150m north of Vernazza's train station and weaves its way through olive groves and terraced gardens for around 2km.

Grind Pesto & Sip Wine

COOKING CLASSES

MAP: 2 P92 **E2**

Minimising the travel miles between pasture and plate, Ligurian cooking is legendary for its unadorned simplicity and Vernazza is, arguably, the best place in Cinque Terre to get involved in local cooking and tasting experiences. **Cinque Sensi** *(5sensivernazza.com; from €50)* offers excellent pesto-making and wine-tasting classes in an attractive grey-stone bar-restaurant building a few steps from the train station. Book in advance.

Buy Street Food in Via Visconti

TAKEAWAY FOOD

MAP: 3 P92 **C3**

It's worth braving the crowds in Via Visconti to sample one or more of the various eating establishments that sell a wide selection of only-in-Liguria street food. Gelato is a Cinque Terre rite of passage, and harbourside Il Porticciolo (p96) sets a high bar with boldly original flavours. Focaccia is the domain of **Batti Batti** (p96), a shop where thick, crispy slices are dispatched with professional speed. The same business maintains a small friggitoria a few doors down, funnelling generous scoops of fried seafood into paper cones.

2011 FLOODS

The 25 October 2011 is a day that will live in infamy in Cinque Terre, especially Vernazza, when biblical floods inundated the village and turned Via Roma into a raging torrent of mud and debris that destroyed the ground floors of practically every building in town. Tragically three people were killed in the destruction and the whole population had to be temporarily evacuated. When the weather had settled, a long slow clean-up began with repairs estimated at around €100 million.

LISTINGS

Best Places for...

€ Budget €€ Midrange €€€ Top End

See p92 for map of locations

Eating

Street Food

Batti Batti €
see 3 C3
This takeaway-only bakery dispatches the best focaccia slices in the village (some would say in Cinque Terre), along with bountifully topped pizza. *10am-6pm Thu-Tue*

Batti Batti Friggitoria €
4 C3
A few shops east from its focaccia outlet, Batti Batti runs an equally casual fried fish shop serving up heaped cones filled with a crispy mix of battered calamari, anchovies, prawns and cod. Chips are also available. *10am-6pm Thu-Tue*

Pippo a Vernazza €
5 E1
A top-of-the-town takeaway located well away from the milling crowds, Pippo offers pasta boxes, homemade desserts and multiple varieties of stuffed focaccia. Grab some to go and have a picnic beside Vernazza's Reggio sanctuary. *11.30am-8pm Thu-Tue*

Ice Cream

Gelateria Vernazza €
6 D3
A crowded-for-a-reason gelato outlet on the main drag offering enticing flavours like ricotta and fig, and white chocolate and raspberry. Good affogato too. *10am-11.30pm*

Il Porticciolo €
7 B3
All-natural gelato in fruity flavours, including Greek yoghurt and honey, right next to Vernazza's harbour. The pale-green pistachio has a dedicated following. *10am-7.30pm*

Fine Dining

Belforte €€€
8 B3
A Vernazza classic for more than 50 years, Belforte serves beautifully prepared seafood dishes in an 11th-century castle. You can fine-dine in the atmospheric stone-walled interior or enjoy the breezy views from one of the terraces. *noon-3pm & 7-10pm Wed-Mon*

La Torre €€€
9 E4
Tucked along a hillside pathway just outside of the centre, La Torre prepares Genovese-style *trofie al pesto* (short, twisted noodles with pesto), seafood spaghetti, stuffed mussels and other classic fare, though the real attraction is the stunning view from the long, narrow terrace. *noon-4pm & 6-10pm*

Morning Munchies

Il Pirata delle 5 Terre €
10 E1
Simple but also superb, the 'pirate' is known for its memorable breakfasts: coffee and the best melt-in-your-mouth Italian pastries in Liguria. You'll be so impressed, you'll want to come back for lunch and dinner. *7am-7pm Sat-Thu*

Blue Marlin €€

11 D3

With outdoor tables on the main drag, and scattered antiques and a lively soundtrack within, Blue Marlin draws a steady stream of locals and visitors for flaky croissants, scrambled eggs and cappuccinos in the morning. *7am-midnight Thu-Tue*

Local Catch

Gambero Rosso €€

12 C3

If you've been subsisting on focaccia, Gambero's house specials – *tegame di Vernazza* (anchovies with baked potatoes and tomatoes), grilled rock octopus or stuffed mussels – will really hit the spot, and the fresh fish baked in sea salt is outstanding. *noon-3pm & 7-10pm Fri-Wed*

Gianni Franzi €€

13 C3

Traditional Cinque Terre seafood (mussels, seafood ravioli and lemon anchovies) has been served up in this harbourside trattoria since the 1960s. When it comes to seafood this fresh, if it's not broken, don't fix it. The outdoor tables make a magnificent setting. *8am-11pm Thu-Tue*

Drinking

Wine & Beer with Snacks

5 Terre Bistrot

14 D3

Slightly concealed above the chapel along Vernazza's main street, this small wine shop and bar is a fine place to sample some of Cinque Terre's best vintages. You can enjoy local wines and snacks along with quality beers like Weihenstephaner at the outdoor tables in front. *11am-10pm*

Bars by the Harbour

Burgus Bar

15 C3

A charming little hole-in-the-wall, with only a couple of ringside benches overlooking Vernazza's stamp-sized beach. *9.30am-midnight*

Ananasso Bar

16 C2

One of several gastro-hubs on the harbour square, Anannasso broadcasts itself with bright yellow umbrellas from a spot near the church. Head over for coffee, cocktails and relaxing vibes. *8am-11pm*

Shopping

Art From the Artist

Bottega d'Arte

17 D3

Hidden behind a small weather-beaten facade, Bottega d'Arte sells the paintings of Antonio Greco, who spent his childhood in Vernazza. His seascapes and village scenes evoke the magic of Cinque Terre. *10.30am-7pm*

Fashion & Accessories

Il Talismano

18 D3

Beneath the arches just south of the train station, this boutique shop stocks clothes, bags, jewellery, wallets and hats, some sourced locally, others drawn from as far away as Nepal. *10am-7.30pm Tue-Sun*

Bottles & Jars

Enoteca Sciacchetrà

19 D3

This store stocks wines from all over Italy, but its pièce de résistance is the local dessert wine, Sciacchetrà. There's also truffle-infused olive oils, Genovese pesto, lemon candies and plenty more. *10am-7pm*

See p105 for eating, drinking and shopping listings

Explore Corniglia

Corniglia is Cinque Terre's 'quiet' middle village that clings to a sheer-sided headland surrounded by terraced fields and plunging cliffs. It is the only village with no direct sea access, although steep steps lead down to a small cove scattered with paint-peeled rowing boats. The village consists of one narrow street that opens out into two small squares and ends at a clifftop lookout called the Belvedere di Santa Maria. Part of Corniglia's tranquillity is due to its lofty vantage. To reach the village proper on foot from the railway station you must climb a switch-backing brick stairway called the Lardarina. The settlement has Roman roots and its ancient core and timeless streetscape were namechecked in Boccaccio's 14th-century literary tome *The Decameron*.

Getting Around

Walking

The village is small and mostly pedestrianised. It's a 15-minute walk up a long outdoor staircase (the Lardarina) from the train station to Piazzetta Ciapara.

Bus

A shuttle bus runs between Corniglia's train station and the village centre every 15 minutes throughout the day. Fares are included on the Cinque Terre Card.

Car

A quiet road brushes the edge of the village connecting it to San Bernardino and beyond, but it's mostly used by locals. Parking is limited.

THE BEST

GELATO
Alberto Gelateria (p105)

TABLE SERVICE
Ristorante Cecio (p105)

NUTELLA CAKE
Pan e Vin (p105)

APERITIF WITH A VIEW
Bar Terza Terre (p105)

VILLAGE ESCAPE
San Bernardino (p103)

Corniglia
ZHAROV PAVEL/SHUTTERSTOCK ©

Walk Corniglia

Advanced navigational skills aren't necessary in tiny Corniglia, a village whose 150 inhabitants live on or abutting one main street. On this short but whimsical wander you'll get a chance to say buongiorno to most of them as they hang out their washing, kick a football around or pull their boats into the marina.

START	END	LENGTH
Scalinata Lardarina	Belvedere di Santa Maria	800m; one hour

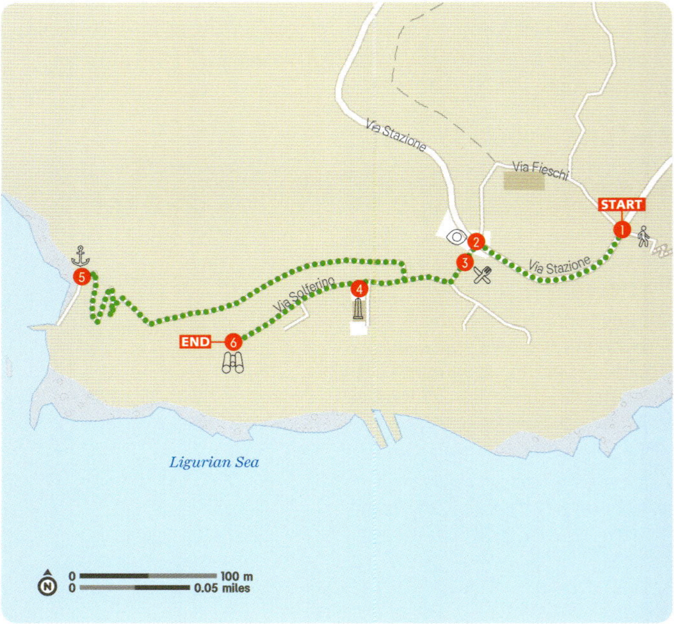

1 Stairway to Heaven

Start at the top of the **Scalinata Lardarina**, a 377-step terracotta-brick stairway. In the days when the Manarola–Corniglia section of the Sentiero Verde-Azzurro (SVA) was open, the stairs formed part of the path. The shallow steps zigzag up the side of the 100m-tall cliff. There's a bird's-eye view of the village station below.

2 Peaceful Piazza

Follow the road around to the tiny **Piazzetta Ciapara** at the entrance to Corniglia. While many hikers pass quickly through, it's an ideal place to slow down and contemplate the nuances of village life. There are several shaded benches, a couple of small grocery stores for refreshments, and an old wine press in the centre of the square – a remnant of Corniglia's once pivotal wine industry.

3 Main Street

Corniglia is a one-street village. The main drag, **Via Fieschi**, is narrow and winding with four-storey houses blocking out the sunlight. Numerous shops and street-food joints will slacken your progress.

4 Village Vantage

The epicentre of Corniglia, the cramped **Largo Taragio** (p104) is filled with competing cafe tables that provide a fine vantage point for the passing parade of villagers and tourists. In the centre stands a war memorial and a small oratory dedicated to St Catherine and the Virgin Mary.

5 Descend to the Sea

A stairway branching off Largo Taragio leads down to a backstreet that descends via numerous steps to Corniglia's oft-forgotten **marina**, little more than a concrete slipway in a rocky cove where paint-peeled rowing boats defy the elements. Confident swimmers sometimes take a dip here if the sea is calm.

6 Clifftop Panorama

Return to the Largo Taragio and continue west along Via Fieschi, which ends another 80m further on at Corniglia's most impressive lookout, **Belvedere di Santa Maria** (p104). From here, you'll have a magnificent 180-degree view along the coast, from the southernmost Cinque Terre village of Riomaggiore up to the forest-covered peninsula of Punta Mesco in the northwest.

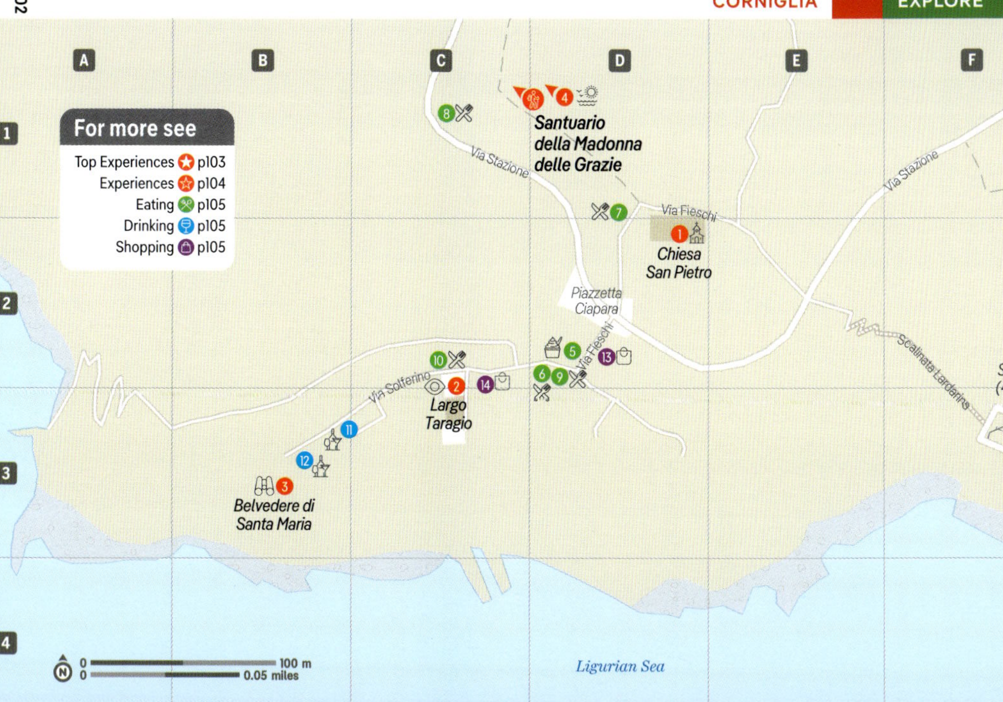
For more see
Top Experiences p103
Experiences p104
Eating p105
Drinking p105
Shopping p105
Santuario della Madonna delle Grazie
Chiesa San Pietro
Piazzetta Ciapara
Largo Taragio
Belvedere di Santa Maria
Via Stazione
Via Fieschi
Via Solferino
Scalinata Lardarina
Station (400m)
Ligurian Sea
100 m
0.05 miles

★ TOP EXPERIENCE

San Bernardino & its Sanctuary

From the main square in Corniglia, you'll spot another small settlement and church outlined on a ridgetop high above the sea. The village is San Bernardino, and the church is the Santuario della Madonna delle Grazie, one of five venerated religious shrines associated with Cinque Terre.

MAP P102 **D1**

PLANNING TIP
For a perfect day trip, hike up to San Bernardino from Corniglia, descend to Vernazza on trail 507, and complete the triangle by walking back to Corniglia on the SVA.

The Church

The Grazie (its name means 'Our Lady of Grace') is substantially newer than the region's other Marian shrines. The current structure, while distinctly traditional in style, dates from the early 1900s when it was built on the site of an erstwhile 16th-century chapel. Older than the existing church is a painting of the Madonna above the altar flanked by ovals of San Bernardo da Chiaravalle and San Bernardino da Siena.

The Village

San Bernardino is a blissfully tranquil hamlet barely touched by tourism. Its only business is a sporadically open bar-shop. The broad open terrace in front of the church offers a fantastic panorama of the coast with the clustered houses of Corniglia nestled far below.

The Paths

There are several ways to reach the sanctuary from Corniglia. The simplest is to follow the main paved road which ascends for 3.3km, hair-pinning its way around the hillside. More relaxing is to take the SVA trail west as far as Prevo, before cutting up to the road and diverting right onto trail 507 (which originates in Vernazza) for the final section.

Scan for information on the sanctuary.

EXPERIENCES

Admire Cinque Terre's Finest Church

CHURCH

MAP: 1 P102 **D2**

Despite its diminutive size, Corniglia harbours the region's most impressive church, **Chiesa San Pietro**, a small Gothic structure whose grey stone facade is embellished by a lattice-like Carrara-marble rose window and a small statue of a key-wielding St Peter flanked by two figures above the entrance.

The interior is awash with lucid baroque frescoes, an elaborately crafted altarpiece and more sombre 18th-century paintings. The church, which stands on a raised terrace above the village, was built in 1334. Its hushed interior is a blissful spot if you've just trudged in off the SVA trail. Enjoy the silence.

FABLED GUVANO BEACH

MAP: 4 P102 **D1**

Spiaggia di Guvano between Corniglia and Vernazza was once a famous nudist spot from the 1960s to the 1990s, when adventurous sunbathers – invariably hippies and free spirits – would hike in via a dark, abandoned railway tunnel. Unfortunately landslides led to the tunnel's closure in 2016, making the beach only accessible by sea to keen kayakers and people on private boat tours. In more recent years, the area has been deemed high risk for mudslides and landslides, and rendered technically out of bounds. For the time being at least, Cinque Terre's most famous beach is closed.

Look Out Over the Sea

VIEWPOINTS

Corniglia's clifftop location offers excellent vantage over the surrounding landscape. Behind the oratory in **Largo Taragio** (MAP: 2 P102 **C2**) there's a small, raised piazza used by local children as a football pitch. The back wall of the oratory has a tiny goal painted on it while the opposite sea-facing wall is topped by a large net designed to catch stray balls. On top of its sporting credentials, the piazza acts as a spectacular viewpoint: through the weathered net you can admire a fine sweep of coastline to the southeast with verdant green hills arcing down towards Manarola perched over the water.

Even better vistas can be enjoyed at the **Belvedere di Santa Maria** (MAP: 3 P102 **B3**) at the southern end of Via Fieschi where the pedestrian street terminates abruptly at a walled terrace given over to the Bar Terza Terra (p105), where enamoured drinkers chink glasses and pinch themselves to check they're not dreaming. Gravitate here for a sundowner.

See p102 for map of locations

Best Places for...

€ Budget €€ Midrange €€€ Top End

Eating

Casual & Takeaway

Alberto Gelateria €
5 D2
Often touted as the best ice cream in the five villages, Alberto's uses local herbs to augment its fruity flavours. The basil from the garden gelato is very good. *10am-10pm*

Pan e Vin €
6 D3
Friendly staff serve up hearty breakfasts, focaccia sandwiches, wine and the best Nutella cake on the Riviera. Squeeze into a church-sized pew and enjoy an elongated *pausa*. *7am-8pm*

À Cáneva €
7 D1
Perfect for breakfast or lunch in a quiet spot beneath the church, Cáneva serves the best pistachio croissant and coffee combo in the five towns. *7am-9pm Mon-Fri, to midnight Sat & Sun*

Ligurian Food

Ristorante Cecio €€
8 C1
Large portions of fish, risotto and pasta served by staff who'll treat you like family. The seafood is epic. *noon-3pm & 6.30-10pm*

Enoteca Il Pirun €€
9 D2
Spread across two floors of a village house, Pirun is a trad trattoria-wine bar with earthy Cinque Terre classics. *noon-3pm & 7-10pm*

Il Buongustaio €€
10 C2
With tables in the main square or inside with views over wine terraces, Buongustaio presents *cucina casalinga* (home cooking), most of it from the sea. *noon-10pm*

Drinking

Cocktails & Aperitifs

La Scuna

11 B3
Craft beer on draft, first-rate cocktails and creative appetisers are a match made in heaven in this surprisingly hip spot in otherwise traditional Corniglia. *8.30am-11.30pm*

Bar Terza Terra
12 B3
Aperitivo combinations with bread, pesto and anchovies on a 100m-high terrace that, after three drinks, makes you feel as if you're flying above the Med. *noon-11pm*

Shopping

Fashion & Souvenirs

Profumo di Mare
13 D2
Souvenir shop with locally made ceramics, handmade jewellery, olive oils and olive-wood cutting boards from upper Liguria. *9am-7pm*

Lanapo
14 C2
Boutique with Milanese connections lends Corniglia a little panache with its handcrafted Cinque Terre sandals and other à la mode footwear. *9am-1pm Mon-Fri, 10am-1pm & 3-7pm Sat*

WALKING TOUR

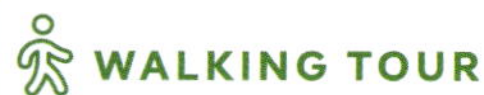

Walk Manarola to Corniglia

An ancient route, part of which has existed since Roman times, this path has replaced the Manarola–Corniglia section of the Sentiero Verde-Azzurro which was damaged by landslides in 2013. Climbing copious steps to the village of Volastra, 335m above sea level, it traverses Cinque Terre's most cherished terraced vineyards before descending into charming Corniglia.

START	END	LENGTH
Manarola	Corniglia	5.4km; 2½ hours

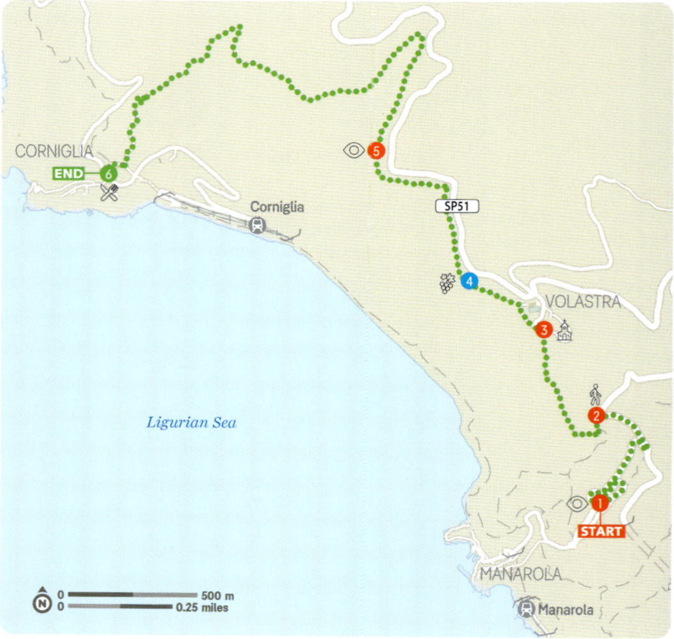

1 Arrivederci Manarola

Head uphill along Manarola's main street, **Via Discovolo**. From the village car park follow the path to the right, with a makeshift sign indicating 'Volastra'. The lane briefly joins a road that wraps around the terraced vineyards above town, depositing you at the foot of some ominous stairs.

2 Heading Upstairs

There are allegedly 1200 **shallow steps** between the road and your arrival in Volastra. Fortunately the stone path is solid and well maintained as it ascends past fig trees, olive groves and old stone walls, steepening slightly as it approaches the pastel houses of the village.

3 Roman Roots

Predating Manarola by at least a millennium, **Volastra** was probably founded by the Romans, although some historians suggest its circular layout is Etruscan. Its name is derived from *'vicus oleaster'* meaning 'country of the olive trees'. Located at 335m above sea level it was – and still is – an important trail nexus and wine-producing area. You can get refreshments at the village shop and find peace in the local church, one of Cinque Terre's five Marian sanctuaries.

4 Straight from the Vine

Just west of Volastra, Italy's most invitingly situated winery, **Cantina Capellini** (p117), is open for wine-tasting most days. Purchase your preferred local tipple from the rustic stall and slump down at a barrel table to enjoy a view of vine terraces falling away to the sea, Manarola on one side, Corniglia on the other.

5 Pine Forest

The ultra-skinny path continues its western traverse, skirting vineyards before passing through someone's sea-facing backyard in the hamlet of **Porciana**. Here, vines give way to former agricultural terraces that have been reclaimed by maritime pine forest. The coastal views are distractingly beautiful. Watch your step!

6 Buongiorno Corniglia

The steep descent begins soon after the junction with path 587 and gets steeper as you near **Corniglia**. Roughly eroded steps eventually lead down to a T-junction. Turn right and follow the lane onto Via Fieschi, Corniglia's main street. At walk's end, treat yourself to appetisers and drinks with a view at La Scuna.

See p116
for eating,
drinking and
shopping
listings

Explore Manarola

Manarola is Cinque Terre's wine village, with vineyards crammed onto narrow terraces high above the settlement. It's also known for its illuminated Christmas nativity scene, ensemble of cosy cafes and bulging wraparound viewpoint, Punta Bonfiglio, with vistas that unfold in both directions along the coast. The image of the town from the Punta, with its multicoloured houses stacked steeply above the harbour, is the region's most ubiquitous photo.

Evidence suggests Manarola is Cinque Terre's oldest village, founded by people from nearby Volastra in medieval times. Its small size and narrow main street, Via Discovolo, means it can get crowded in summer. Tourists aside, Manarola has retained its authenticity and local people (population 353) still speak a distinctive dialect, different from the other four villages.

Getting Around

Walking

Like all the Cinque Terre villages, Manarola is car-free. A tunnel connects the main urban area to the train station. A steep path leads up to Volastra.

Car

There's a car park just outside the village at the top end of Via Discovolo.

Bus

Local buses can take you up to the sanctuary and vineyards in Volastra if you don't fancy walking.

THE BEST

ARTISTIC HEIRLOOM
Tryptich in the Chiesa di San Lorenzo (p111)

LOCAL TRAIL
Via Beccara (p114)

SPOT FOR AN APERITIF
Nessun Dorma (p113)

SEAFOOD RESTAURANT
Trattoria dal Billy (p116)

AFTERNOON COFFEE & CAKE
Cappun Magru (p116)

Manarola

WALKING TOUR

Walk Manarola

Manarola is small and compact. Its simple layout is arranged around its one main street, Via Discovolo, that connects two diminutive squares and a salty harbour. This short stroll captures the village's underlying essence, from restaurants serving food grown on farmed terraces to fishing boats pulled up in the harbour.

START	END	LENGTH
Manarola train station	Harbour	1km; 45 minutes

1 Main Street Stroll

Take the pedestrian tunnel that leads from the station to the village. As you emerge into the light, turn right. The winding lane **Via Discovolo**, named after the 20th-century Italian painter Antonio Discovolo, is the commercial artery of Manarola. Food shops, clothing stores and snack stands jockey for attention as locals and tourists mill past.

2 Ecclesial Heartbeat

It's a steady uphill climb as you follow the sharp curve in the road. Shortly after the bend you'll reach the **Chiesa di San Lorenzo**, a stolid 14th-century Ligurian-Gothic church. It's notable for the 14th-century triptych on the altar depicting the Madonna with Child, St Catherine and St Lawrence.

3 Around the Church

Just opposite the church is a **bell tower**. This also served as a lookout post during the 14th century. A marble memorial above the door pays homage to the villagers who lost their lives in WWI. Stroll to the side of the tower for a partial view of the steeply terraced vineyards rising above town.

4 Backstreet Diversion

Continue on and climb the set of stairs leading up to your right. The narrow lane **Via Rollandi** takes you past village homes and one of Manarola's best restaurants (Trattoria dal Billy, p116), while offering fine views over the terraces. Continue almost to the end then take the Scalinata Pezzali back down to the main street and turn right.

5 Main Square Mosaic

Manarola's **Piazza Dario Capellini** is relatively austere, save for a large mosaic etched onto the pavestones depicting fish and seabirds. Slightly raised from the surrounding streets, it offers a good sense of the vertical nature of the village, with hillslopes and tall houses rising steeply on both sides.

6 Meet the Sea

Turn left and walk down to Manarola's petite **harbour**. You can zigzag your way down to the water's edge for a prime view of the Mediterranean. Although there's no beach here, a few hardy swimmers go for dips in the deep water just off the dock. Others sunbathe on the rocks fringing the shore.

Punta Bonfiglio
Nessun Dorma
Ligurian Sea
Harbour
Via di Corniglia
Piazza Dario Capellini
Via Antonio Discovolo
Via Birolli
Via Belvedere
Via Rollandi
Tunnel
Piazzale Papa Innocenzo IV
Chiesa di San Lorenzo
Oratorio dei Disciplinanti
Arbaspàa
SP370
Via Beccara
Manarola

For more see

Experiences p113
Eating p116
Drinking p117
Shopping p117

0 200 m
0 0.1 miles

EXPERIENCES

Relish Pesto & Wine at Nessun Dorma

FOOD & DRINK

MAP: 1 P112 **A2**

On the wave-kissed Bonfiglio promontory overlooking the pastel-coloured houses of Manarola, **Nessun Dorma** *(nessundormacinqueterre.com)* is a leafy terrace bar that makes a magical setting for a sundowner. There's a great wine selection and plenty of creative cocktails (try a *limoncino spritz*) that pair well with sandwiches, salads, bruschette and cheese platters.

Not surprisingly, it's boisterously popular. To reserve a space in the perennial queue, register through its online app. You can enhance the experience by booking an inhouse pesto-making class, which includes dinner and wine-tasting.

Pause in Piazzale Papa Innocenzo IV

SQUARE

The ecclesial hub of Manarola is dominated by two churches guarded by a separate bell tower that was once used as a defensive lookout. The **Chiesa di San Lorenzo** (MAP: 2 P112 **D2**) is the main village church dating from 1338. It houses a 14th-century triptych. The smaller, more austere **Oratorio dei Disciplinanti** (MAP: 3 P112 **D2**) hails from the 15th century and is almost identical to its namesake in Corniglia.

When the tourists head home, the tiny **Piazzale Papa Innocenzo IV** (MAP: 4 P112 **D2**) often becomes an impromptu football pitch. This is an ideal time to visit. The cosily cramped Cappun Magru (p116) nearby is a perfect spot for a post-hike sandwich.

The square is named after the 13th-century pope, Innocent IV, rumoured to have been born in Manarola in around 1195 (other sources claim he was born in Genoa). He reigned as pope for 11 years between 1243 and 1254.

Trek Uphill to a Sanctuary

CHURCH & HIKE

MAP: 5 P112 **F1**

Manarola's out-of-village **Santuario della Madonna delle Salute** stands at the top end of Volastra, a 45-minute walk from Manarola up copious steps, and dates from the 13th century. The simple Romanesque-Gothic structure is made from local sandstone and, in common with other Cinque Terre churches, guards a venerated image of the Madonna (Our Lady of Health) mounted behind the altar. According to legend, the church bells were buried underground during Saracen raids, and never recovered. It is said that they still toll on stormy nights.

The sanctuary makes a peaceful waystation on the walk between Manarola and Corniglia.

Attempt the Tougher Alternative to Via dell'Amore

HIKE

MAP: 6 P112 **F4**

Before the Via dell'Amore (Path of Love) was carved into the cliffside in the 1920s, the only non-rail land-link between Manarola and Riomaggiore was **Via Beccara**, a tough, energy-sapping climb up and over the Costa Corniolo, a steep headland that separates the two villages.

Numbered as trail 531 on signposts, the path ascends almost vertically via steps through terraced gardens to a lofty viewpoint whereupon it descends in an equally precipitous manner on the other side. The distance is just under 1.5km but most people take at least an hour to complete it. Notwithstanding, the scenery is stupendous – easily as good as the Via dell'Amore – but without the incessant crowds or payment system.

Via Beccara was reincarnated as the main Manarola–Riomaggiore path between 2012 and 2024 when the Via dell'Amore was closed after a landslide.

It starts opposite the church in Manarola's Piazzale Papa Innocenzo IV.

View Punta Bonfiglio

VIEWPOINT

MAP: 7 P112 **A2**

Manarola's prized viewpoint, **Punta Bonfiglio**, occupies a rocky promontory that sticks out into the Mediterranean. The lovely panorama back towards the village is one of Cinque Terre's most recognisable vistas. A path curves around the Punta's lower skirts before dead-ending on the western side with a railing to protect from the steep drop-off. From here, the erstwhile Sentiero Azzurro to Corniglia is still visible etched into the hillside. This part of the path has been closed since landslides in 2013. There are currently no plans to reopen

NATIVITY SCENE

Every year between early December and mid-January, diminutive Manarola is the improbable home to the largest lit *Presepe* (Nativity scene) in the world. Set up in the vineyards above the village, the scene covers 4000 sq metres and uses 12km of cable to light over 300 figures. The project was conceived and put together piecemeal by former railway worker Mario Andreoli beginning in 1961, and in recent years has incorporated recycled materials and solar power into the mix. The lights are clearly visible from the sea, or you can view them more closely from Manarola's main square, Piazzale Papa Innocenzo IV.

LOCAL WINES

Cinque Terre is a legally protected DOC wine region that produces crisp, intense white wines made from grapes grown on the steep terraces around the five villages, particularly Manarola. The most famous variety is Sciacchetrà, concocted from a mix of Bosco, Albarola and Vermentino grapes that are dried off the vine for two months before being pressed and fermented. The resulting sweet *passito* wine is well-known as a dessert wine but can also be paired with cheese. Sciacchetrà is an expensive wine, so locals usually save a bottle for special occasions.

it. A higher alternative route to Corniglia heads west via Volastra.

On the bluff's beautifully landscaped upper level, a rest area, including a kids' playground, has been constructed, with Cinque Terre's ultimate aperitif bar, Nessun Dorma (p113) , sitting just below. Nearby are the ruins of an old chapel once used as a shelter by local farmers.

Savour a Sunset Cruise BOAT TRIP

MAP: 8 P112 C2

With one side facing the Mediterranean and the other clinging to land, you've only really seen half of Cinque Terre's villages until you've admired them from the sea. Manarola is the HQ for **Arbaspàa** *(arbaspaa.com)*, arguably Cinque Terre's finest travel agency.

Among their litany of tours are several unique boat trips. Staffed by multilingual guides, they offer a vast range of activities, including wine-tasting at a local vineyard, boat trips, kayaking excursions, photography tours, hiking trips and more.

Departing daily between April and October from Manarola's cute harbour, its sunset cruises explore grottos, caves and cliffs everywhere between Riomaggiore and Monterosso.

Wine is available on board. Take one of their afternoon boat tours and you'll get a chance to add snorkelling in the marine park into the bargain (weather permitting).

The company hires out apartments in all the Cinque Terre villages and also runs an outdoor shop-cum-activity centre called **Explora** (p117) located in Via Discovolo. Arbaspàa has a deep commitment to sustainability and its founders helped create the nonprofit Fondazione Manarola, which helps rebuild the dry-stone walls around the village.

LISTINGS

Best Places for...

€ Budget €€ Midrange €€€ Top End

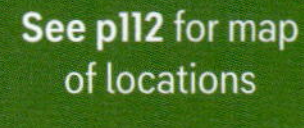
See p112 for map of locations

Eating

Seafood

Trattoria dal Billy €€
9 C3
Hidden off a narrow lane in the upper reaches of Manarola, Billy's fires up some of the best food in Cinque Terre. It's fish all the way – grilled, baked, fried or raw. On clear days, book a table on the terrace for superb views. Reservations essential. *noon-3pm & 6-10pm Fri-Wed*

Da Aristide €€
 C2
Sit at tables in an old village house or pews in a bright, modern marquee terrace on the square and order generous plates of stuffed anchovies or lemon-doused grilled octopus to share. *noon-3pm & 7-10pm*

Il Porticciolo €€
 B2
The 'little port' is a football kick away from Manarola's harbour and serves the fruits of the sea in a salubrious streetside conservatory. Try the octopus or the *vongole* (clams). *noon-3pm & 6.30-9pm Thu-Tue*

Trattoria La Scogliera €€
 C3
Popular with the tourist hordes, Scogliera has a pleasant stone interior and bright front glass-windowed awning. It specialises in seafood with a back-up of pesto pasta and pizza. *11am-11pm Sat-Thu*

Locanda Tiabuscion €€€
 E1
An away-from-the-crowds gourmet surprise in the hamlet of Volastra high above Manarola, Tiabuscion is worth a steep walk up several hundred steps for its spectacular seafood-on-the-terrace experience featuring prawns, clams and a formidable antipasti plate. *10.30am-10.30pm Tue-Sun*

Super Snacks

Cappun Magru €
14 D1
Diminutive cafe next to Manarola's church that sings out for a post-hike sandwich – the seafood *panini* are excellent, ditto the sugar-boosting dessert tarts. *9.30am-6pm Tue-Sun*

Nessun Dorma – Oficina 231 €
15 C2
Another outlet of Manarola's famous sundowner and pesto-making emporium, the Oficina acts like a mini *panini*-building factory where you can construct chunky sandwiches from a deli-full of local ingredients. *9.30am-7.30pm*

Bar-Gelateria Enrica €
 B3
This cheap and very cheerful catch-all place rustles up ice cream, pizzas, *panini* and other breezy snacks in a handy nook down by the harbour. Tourist trap it isn't. *8.15am-8.30pm Wed-Mon*

Takeaway Pasta €

The nearest Cinque Terre gets to fast food is this fabulous takeaway that has large tubs of handmade pasta including trofie, *pansotti* ravioli and gnocchi. The tiramisu is equally memorable. Despite the name, you can perch at several tables alfresco. *11am-8pm*

Ice Cream

Gelateria 5 Terre

Manarola's contribution to the Cinque Terre ice-cream options advertises all its flavours and cones as gluten- and lactose-free and has several vegan options. It also serves crepes, sorbets and *granite*. *11am-6pm*

Drinking

Wine & Sundowners

Nessun Dorma

On a wave-kissed promontory overlooking Manarola, this leafy terrace is a magical setting for a sundowner accompanied by heavenly *bruschette*. You'll need to book a table through its app to get a space in the queue. *3.30-9pm Wed-Mon*

A Piè de Campu

Serves up excellent wines and superb focaccia on a tree-covered terrace in the upper part of town. During the daytime, you can explore Cinque Terre's unique wines in the tasting room downstairs. It also offers focaccia-making classes with a master baker. *7-10pm Tue-Sun*

Cantina Capellini

Don't under any circumstances miss a relaxing dose of fresh-from-the-vineyard wine-tasting at Cantina Capellini just outside Volastra. Here you can sit on a vine-shaded terrace, grapes within picking distance, and look down on Manarola and Corniglia while sipping Cinque Terre's finest vintages. *11am-7pm*

Local Taverns

La Cantina dello Zio Bramante

Just below street level, this friendly local watering hole is the best place in town for some late-night revelry. There's live music on weekends, good local wines on hand and you can nibble on *bruschette*, sandwiches and other rudimentary snacks. *noon-midnight Fri-Wed*

Shopping

Arts & Crafts

L'Emporio

22 C2

This colourfully decorated shop sells works by local artists and artisans: marine life and lighthouse paintings done on pieces of old fishing boats, nautically themed jewellery and tiny wooden model boats. *9.30am-8.30pm*

Sports & Outdoors

Cinque Terre Trekking

23 C1

If you're eager to get out and do some hiking but didn't bring the right gear, head to this outfitter for all your hiking needs. *11am-1pm & 2-7pm Wed-Mon*

Explora

24 C2

Small shop that stocks handy essentials for outdoor adventures, as well as trail maps and a few books on Cinque Terre. It also act as a HQ for the Arbaspàa tour company. *9am-1pm & 2-7pm*

See p125
for eating,
drinking and
shopping
listings

Explore Riomaggiore

If Cinque Terre had a HQ, it would probably be Riomaggiore, the closest village to La Spezia by train and the largest in terms of population (around 1500). Its size also means it feels less congested than Manarola and Vernazza, especially if you veer off its arterial street, Via Colombo.

Riomaggiore has a couple of small churches and a ruined castle on a headland overlooking the sea. Most people hang around the marina (accessed through a tunnel) where fishing boats fight salt-rot, and multistorey pastel houses glow romantically at sunset. This is the best place in Cinque Terre to rent a kayak or organise a diving or snorkelling excursion. A short walk to the east brings you to pebbly, wave-battered Spiaggia di Fossola.

Getting Around

Walking

As with the other Cinque Terre villages, Riomaggiore is mostly pedestrianised and walking is the only practical way to get around.

Lifts

There are two lifts to help you navigate Riomaggiore's steep streets, one next to the train station, the other close to the Chiesa di San Giovanni Battista.

Bus

A local bus service links Riomaggiore with several local hamlets, including Volastra.

THE BEST

PLACE FOR A PICNIC
Santuario della Madonna di Montenero (p123)

PLACE TO GET WET
Spiaggia di Fossola (p124)

MARINE LIFE
Secca della Peschiera (p124)

PIZZA JOINT
Pizzeria Kepris (p125)

BAR SERVICE
Vertical Bar (p125)

Riomaggiore

Walk Riomaggiore

On this looping stroll around Cinque Terre's largest village, you'll enjoy marvellous views over the seaside and visit iconic buildings, including a 14th-century church. You'll also get a glimpse of some fading murals, which depict the backbreaking work of Cinque Terre farmers. The walk ends at the village's small, overwhelmingly loved marina.

START	END	LENGTH
Train Station	Marina	3km; 1½ hours

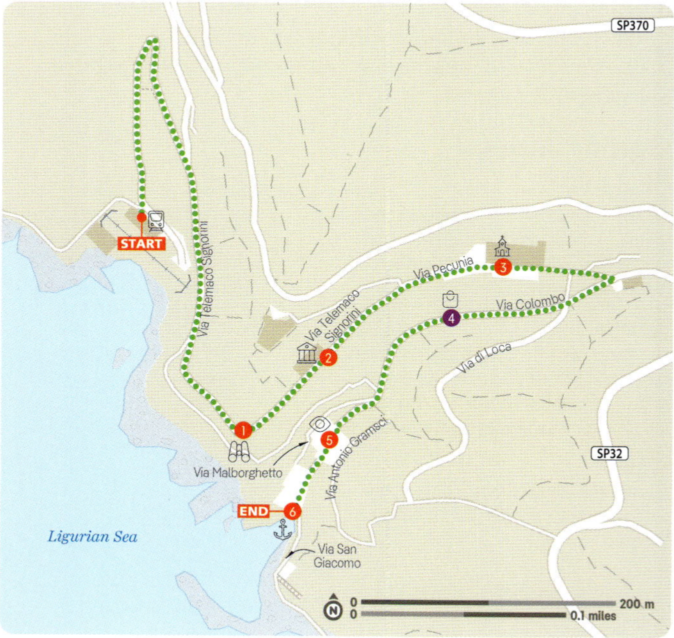

1 Village View

Starting off from the train station, walk uphill (rather than through the tunnel), take the first stairs to your right and continue ascending until you reach a **viewpoint** overlooking the village. Locals gather here on park benches beneath shady palm trees, catching up on gossip against a mesmerising backdrop.

2 City Hall Murals

Keep following the path as it winds up and around, and you'll pass by murals of grape pickers and fishermen above a busty blue sea goddess adorning Riomaggiore's **city hall**. These works, which celebrate two of the town's key industries, were painted by the Argentine-Italian artist Silvio Benedetto (born 1938).

3 Church Perch

The heart of spiritual life in the village, **Chiesa di San Giovanni Battista** occupies a strategic position watching over the town. The 14th-century church is devoted to the town's patron saint, John the Baptist, whose feast day is celebrated with fervour on 24 June each year. After taking in the fine view in front of the church, head along the narrowing lane and turn right on Via Santuario opposite a small oratory.

4 Main Street Action

You'll meet weaving crowds as you walk downhill and enter the commercial centre of Riomaggiore. **Via Colombo** is packed with shops and cafes, with outdoor dining spots offering excellent vantage points of the passing people parade.

5 Crossing the Square

Take Via Colombo to the end, then climb up the stairs on either side. You'll arrive at the sunny **Piazza Vignaioli**, which is another key communal spot in Riomaggiore. Kids race around the open space, beneath the tall pastel-hued buildings framing the square trying to punt footballs around the oblivious tourists.

6 Meet the Sea

Head back down the stairs, and descend another set of stairs to head down to the sea. Riomaggiore's tiny waterfront **marina** has just a couple of restaurants and is sometimes full of boats. During bad weather, locals haul their watercraft out of the sea and onto the sloping concrete.

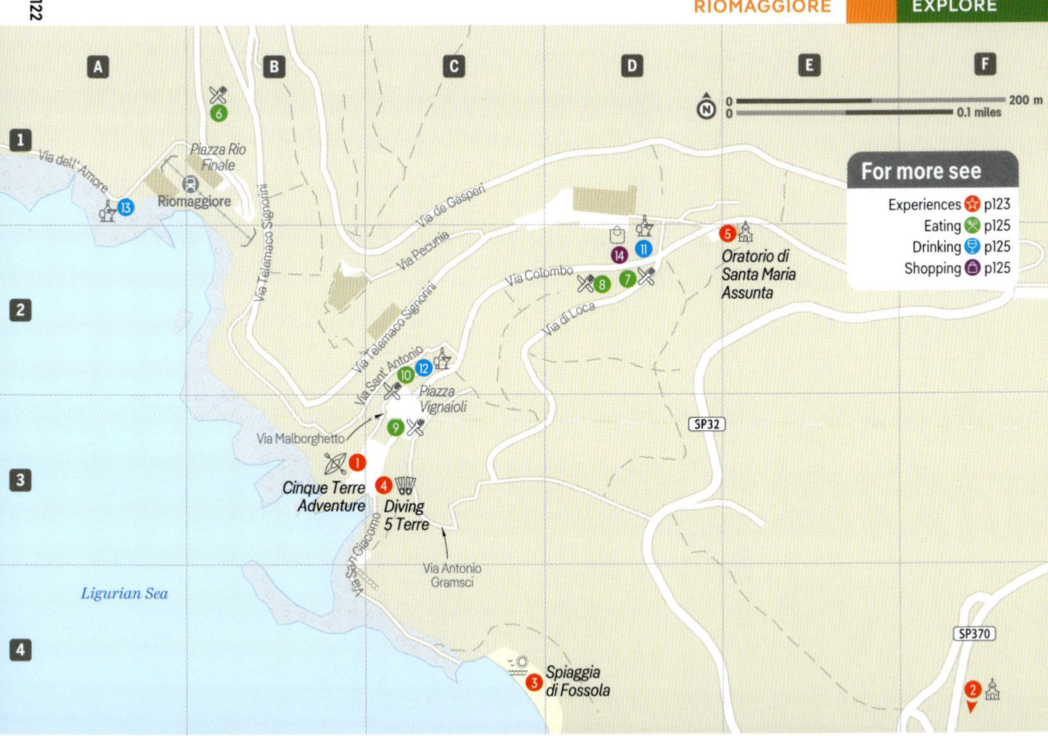
For more see
Experiences p123
Eating p125
Drinking p125
Shopping p125
200 m
0.1 miles
Via dell'Amore
Piazza Rio Finale
Riomaggiore
Via Telemaco Signorini
Via de Gasperi
Via Pecunia
Via Colombo
Via di Loca
Via Sant' Antonio
Piazza Vignaioli
Via Malborghetto
Cinque Terre Adventure
Diving 5 Terre
Via San Giacomo
Via Antonio Gramsci
Oratorio di Santa Maria Assunta
SP32
SP370
Ligurian Sea
Spiaggia di Fossola

EXPERIENCES

Kayak the Coast
KAYAKING

MAP: 1 P122 **B3**

Laced with caves and beaches, some of which are only accessible by boat, Cinque Terre lends itself to kayaking and stand-up paddleboarding. When the seas are cooperating, it's possible to visit all five towns in a day and even indulge in some supervised cliff-jumping. Riomaggiore is the best launch point and has a good rental outlet, **Cinque Terre Adventure** *(cinqueterreadventure.com; rental from €10 per hour)*, in the marina. Guided trips are also offered.

Join the Sanctuary Circuit
CHURCH & HIKE

MAP: 2 P122 **F4**

Of Cinque Terre's five main sanctuaries (one for each village), Riomaggiore's **Santuario della Madonna di Montenero** is the most spectacularly sited. Occupying a pine-fringed meadow atop a steep promontory overlooking the Mediterranean, its terracotta bell tower and arched white facade is visible for miles around. While a church has stood here since at least 1335, the current structure was expanded and upgraded in the 18th and 19th centuries. Its frescoed interior is rarely open, but the attractive surroundings make a fabulous spot for a picnic.

The sanctuary can be incorporated in a circular walk from Riomaggiore starting in the marina on trail 593V and ascending steep steps past walled gardens to a main road (SP370). From here, another steep path makes a final climb to the hilltop sanctuary located at an elevation of 340m. Complete the loop on trail 593 as it descends more gently around a ravine back into the top end of Riomaggiore.

LONGER WALKS FROM RIOMAGGIORE

Colle Telegrafo This waystation on the AV5T with an inviting bar-restaurant makes a good turnaround point for a 9km round-trip walk. Hike up to the Montenero sanctuary first before continuing on trail 593. • **Porto Venere** From Telegrafo, it's possible to continue hiking east as far as Porto Venere (5km) doing the AV5T in reverse. You can return to Riomaggiore by a combination of bus and train. • **Sella La Croce** Tough 2.4km climb to a saddle on the AV5T through vineyards and orchards and, later, chestnut and pine forest. It's marked trail 501 and graded EE (for expert hikers).

NATIONAL PARK INFO

Riomaggiore and the whole Cinque Terre area is part of the **Parco Nazionale delle Cinque Terre** *(parconazionale5terre.it)*. Park authorities maintain the various hiking trails that surround the five villages and preserve the surrounding seas which are included in a protected marine area. The useful park website is worth visiting when planning your trip, or there are information points at each Cinque Terre train station and in La Spezia. You can buy Cinque Terre Trekking Cards online, at the info offices, or at entrance booths on the SVA trail.

Romance on Fossola Beach — BEACH

MAP: 3 P122 C4

Rough, rugged and delightfully secluded, this rocky cove at **Spiaggia di Fossola** is the polar opposite of the classic Riviera beach. There are no private beach clubs and no neat lines of umbrellas and sun-loungers. The small pebble and rock beach, often lashed by powerful waves, is reached by a short concrete trail southeast of Riomaggiore marina. Framed by steep hillsides and backed by a reinforced wall, it's an elemental place that was once extolled as the most romantic beach in Europe. Swimmers should be wary of strong currents.

Dip Underwater in a Marine Park — DIVING

MAP: 4 P122 C3

Parco Nazionale delle Cinque Terre has a sub-aquatic side. The waters offshore are part of a marine park with three levels of protection that places restrictions on motorboats, fishing and swimming. Access is through Riomaggiore, which is home to the area's only dive-center, **Diving 5 Terre** *(5terrediving.it)* located in the harbour. There are several dive sites in the vicinity, at least one of which is reachable directly from the shore.

Secca della Peschiera is just off Spiaggia di Fossola, and rocks protruding from the seabed attract octopuses, crabs and anemones. Immersions, courses and rentals can be organised through Diving 5 Terre.

Stop by the Oratorio di Santa Maria Assunta — CHURCH

MAP: 5 P122 E2

Built by the Disciplinati, a Christian brotherhood in the 16th century, the **Oratorio di Santa Maria Assunta** is a simple stone church with a rust-red bell tower provides an atmospheric diversion for hikers and restaurant-hunters strolling along Via Colombo. It's home to an unusual 14th-century wooden tempera triptych, the *Madonna delle catene (Madonna of the Chains)* depicting the Mother of God standing over chains. It's meant to represent the kidnapping and enslavement of coastal inhabitants by Barbary pirates who raided the coast over the years. The artist is unknown. Back in the day, the brothers would gather here to recite hymns and chant to the Madonna.

Best Places for...

See p122 for map of locations

€ Budget €€ Midrange €€€ Top End

Eating

Quick-Fire Pizza

Pizzeria Kepris €
6 B1
This hole-in-the-wall next to Riomaggiore station has become the unlikely Pavarotti of Cinque Terre pizza. Anything with pesto on it is good. *noon-2.30pm & 6-9.30pm Thu-Tue*

Veciu Muin €€
7 D2
Italian restaurant on Riomaggiore's main drag with a reasonably priced mix of pizzas, pastas and main courses served quickly. *11.30am-11.30pm Mon-Sat*

Meat Specialists

La Cantina del Macellaio €€
8 D2
In seafood-centric Cinque Terre, the Macellaio serves Turin-worthy braised beef and pasta with wild boar, plus burgers, ribs and cured hams. *7-11pm Mon-Sat*

Ligurian Classics

Rio Bistrot €€
9 C3
Small, romantic, harbour-side nook that is rated as one of Riomaggiore's top dining destinations. Bank on beautifully prepared seafood dishes, attentive service and an elegant setting. *12.30-3pm & 7-10.30pm Tue-Sun*

La Lampara €€€
10 C2
Enjoy classy local dishes (fish predominates) or stay simple with pizza and pesto. The hungry should opt for the four-course tasting menu. *noon-2.30pm & 7-11pm Wed-Mon*

Drinking

Bars for Every Mood

Vertical Bar
11 D2
With outdoor tables on Riomaggiore's main drag, the Vertical is ground zero for coffee or cocktails. Has great music, mellow vibes and excellent people-analysing. *11am-11.30pm*

Bar O'Netto
12 C2
Over 100 years old and about as local as you can get in Riomaggiore, O'Netta serves beer and wine with complimentary snacks in a lively drinking den replete with village banter. *7am-1am*

A Pié de Mà
13 A1
A delightful spot for an afternoon pick-me-up, on a terrace. Serves local craft beers as well as coffees, a few desserts and a fine selection of wines from Cinque Terre. *11am-10pm Wed-Mon*

Shopping

Food & Drink

Enoteca d'uu Scintu
14 D2
This is *the* place for Genovese pesto, extra virgin olive oils, lemon-scented soaps, pretty bottles of *limoncino*, grappa and wines, plus amaretto biscuits. *9am-10pm*

See p139
for eating,
drinking and
shopping
listings

Explore La Spezia & the Bay of Poets

Heading out from Cinque Terre along the Riviera di Levante you'll find more coastal splendour but without the incessant crowds. To the east, La Spezia was just another Cinque Terre–style fishing village until 1857 when the Italian navy took up residence and the bayside settlement became a major naval base. The modern city is flanked by a handful of attractive seaside villages – San Terenzo, Lerici and Tellaro – that line the east side of the Golfo della Spezia, known more romantically as the Golfo dei Poeti, referencing the likes of Lord Byron, Percy and Mary Shelley and DH Lawrence, who were regular visitors. On the west side of the bay, Porto Venere, backed by rugged cliffs, is sometimes known as Cinque Terre's honorary sixth member.

Getting Around

Train

La Spezia Centrale is a major train hub with regional trains and fast direct services to other parts of Liguria and Italy. Levanto is on the main east–west train line with quick links to Cinque Terre and Genoa.

Bus

For the villages on the Golfo dei Poeti, you'll need to change onto a bus in La Spezia: bus 11 or P for Porto Venere, and bus L or S for Lerici and San Terenzo.

Harbour, La Spezia
KAVALENKAVA/SHUTTERSTOCK ©

THE BEST

CASTLE
Castello Doria (p130)

STREET FOOD
Anciua (p140)

PLACE FOR POETIC MEDITATION
Grotta di Byron (p131)

EVENING STROLL
Passeggiata Morin (p129)

BOHEMIAN BAR
Resilience Cafe (p141)

Walk La Spezia

La Spezia is a hard-working port town that gets routinely overlooked. Most Cinque Terre–bound tourists change trains for Riomaggiore and Manarola without ever leaving the station. Yet the city emits a warm Ligurian air for those keen to see Italy without the frilly wrapping paper. Just turn left out of the station and keep walking.

START	END	LENGTH
La Spezia Centrale Train Station	Porto Mirabello	2½km; three hours

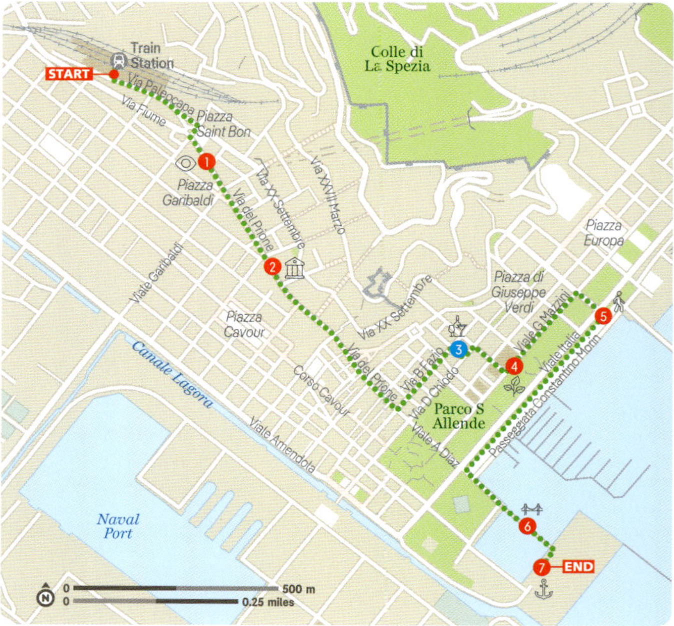

1 Vibrant Via

From the roundabout outside the station, Via Fiume leads southeast, merging with a wide pedestrian lane called **Via del Prione** that curves through the historic centre. This is one of the oldest streets in town and is sprinkled with shops, cafes, restaurants and several museums (plus the tourist office).

2 Fine-Arts Museum

Halfway down Via del Prione, the **Museo Amedeo Lia**, set in a restored 17th-century friary, is La Spezia's star cultural attraction. The collection spans the 13th to 18th centuries and includes paintings by masters such as Tintoretto, Montagna, Titian and Pietro Lorenzetti. Also on show are Roman bronzes and ecclesiastical treasures, such as Limoges crucifixes and illuminated musical manuscripts.

3 Boho Hangout

A wonderfully Riviera-esque spot for a pre- or post-dinner drink, **Resilience Cafe** (p141) exudes effortless style with claret-red walls, generously stuffed bookshelves, glittering chandeliers and vintage furniture. Summon up a slice of cake and a cocktail, or design your own *bruschetta* and cheese 'n' meat board. Talented troubadours strum acoustic sets and there's a leafy street terrace for summer romance.

4 Public Gardens

The salubrious **Giardini Pubblici** are a work of art, dotted with equestrian statues, marble fountains, gazebos and a diverse array of trees. Various signboards explain their layout and history.

5 Promenade Stroll

To see the Spezzini in their natural habitat, come to the wide brick **Passeggiata Morin** overlooking the marina, lined with palm trees and embellished with well-tended flower beds. Evening strollers make for the Molo Italia lighthouse.

6 Port Link

Opened to much fanfare in 2013, the cable-stayed **Ponte Thaon di Revel** pedestrian bridge connects the city with the port. Vaguely resembling a large double-masted sailing ship, the 160m-long structure marks the gateway to La Spezia's port area.

7 Where the Boats Come in

It's worth continuing your stroll on the other side of the Ponte Thaon di Revel for a look at La Spezia's modern, expansive **Porto Mirabello**. You'll see some impressive yachts and pretty views of city, sea and mountainous horizon. It's at its best around sunset.

LA SPEZIA
A
B
C
D
E
F
1
2
3
4
La Spezia Ventrale
Piazza Saint Bon
Piazza Garibaldi
Colle di La Spezia
Via Francesco Crispi
Via Vittorio Veneto
Piazza Europa
Via XXIV Maggio
Largo Fiorillo
Via Filippo Corridoni
Via Venezia
Via Antonio Gramsci
Via Milano
Via Napoli
Via Roma
Via Nino Bixio
Corso Cavour
Viale Amendola
Viale Garibaldi
Via del Prione
Via XX Settembre
Via XXVII Marzo
Castello di San Giorgio
Piazza di Giuseppe Verdi
Via Gramsci
Via Colombo
Via Fratelli Rosselli
Via Urbano Rattazzi
Via Fieschi
Canale Lagora
Piazza Cesare Battisti
Via Sapri
Via Felice Cavallotti
Via Fazio
Via Domenico Chiodo
Via Giovanni Minzoni
Viale Giuseppe Mazzini
Viale Italia
Passeggiata Constantino Morin
Parco S Allende
Viale Armando Diaz
Giardini Pubblicii
Piazza Domenico Chiodo
Museo Tecnico Navale della Spezia
Naval Port
Naval Base
Via Carlo Bertella
0 200 m
0 0.1 miles
For more see
Top Experiences p130
Experiences p133
Eating p139
Drinking p141
Shopping p141

★ TOP EXPERIENCE

Porto Venere

The sun-bleached, seven-storey houses of Porto Venere form an impregnable citadel around the town's Castello Doria, a muscular fort that concertinas up the hillside. Lying on the western tip of the Golfo dei Poeti, the hardy fishing village ambience was a potent muse for British poet Lord Byron.

MAP **P135**

PLANNING TIP
Porto Venere isn't on the train line. Change onto bus 11 or P outside La Spezia Centrale.

Castello Doria

With its grey stone walls looking as imposing as the cliffs on which they stand, Porto Venere's **Castello Doria** is a formidable example of Genoese military architecture. Dating from the 12th century, with an upper section added in the 1450s, it was a highly strategic citadel in its time, and once stood on the front line with Genoa's maritime feud with Pisa. The interior is worth visiting for its fine construction details and expansive views from the terraced gardens, although information panels are scant and there is little in the way of museum exhibits.

The castle connects to the old town walls, which include a medieval gateway that guards the entrance to Porto Venere's *caruggi* (narow streets).

Chiesa di San Pietro

The wave-lashed **Chiesa di San Pietro**, built in 1198 in Gothic style, stands on the ruins of a 5th-century palaeo-Christian church with its extant floor still partially visible. Perched on a bluff with a distinctive medieval Italian striped facade, it looks as if it might have been hewn directly from the rock. Before its Christianisation, the building was a Roman temple dedicated to the goddess Venus, born from the foam of the sea, from whom Porto Venere takes its name.

Scan for more information about the village.

BENNY MARTY/SHUTTERSTOCK ©

Grab a *panini* stuffed with anchovies or pick up a whole spinach pie for a picnic at Anciua, hidden in a narrow alley behind the harbour.

The striped interior is beautiful in its simplicity. Just outside, a small terrace with Romanesque arches frames a glorious view of Cinque Terre's plunging cliffs.

Grotta di Byron

At the end of Porto Venere's quay, a Cinque Terre panorama unfolds from the rocky terraces of a cave formerly known as **Grotta Arpaia** (pictured). British writer Lord Byron used to come here to meditate; beset by affairs, debts and public scandal, he had plenty to think about. A plaque recalls how he once swam across the gulf to San Terenzo to visit the resident Shelleys (a marathon 7km). Despite the cave's collapse, the rocky terraces remain quite beautiful and suitably dishevelled. You can scramble down to what's left of it. Steps and a railing offer some support.

Voyage to the Islands in the Gulf

ISLANDS

MAP: 1 P135 **B3**

Three islands form a small archipelago that juts into the Mediterranean south of Porto Venere. The largest, **Palmaria**, is home to around 50 residents and can be reached from Porto Venere on a ferry. Ringed by towering cliffs, sheltered coves and several rocky beaches, it can be visited as part of a day trip. Palmaria has several old forts and batteries and is covered in vegetation characterised by typical Mediterranean forest and scrub. The path that circumnavigates the island is well signposted and takes about two hours to complete. There's a bar-restaurant where you can chill over a glass of wine afterwards.

The two smaller islands are Tino, home to a lighthouse and a ruined monastery, and tiny Tinetto, which guards the remains of a 5th-century oratory. Both are maintained by the Italian navy and closed to the public.

Take a Lift to La Spezia's Castle

CASTLE & MUSEUM

MAP: 2 P130 **D2**

La Spezia's 14th-century **Castello di San Giorgio** *(museodelcastello.museilaspezia.it; adult/child €6/4.50)* is one of the most impressively intact forts on the Ligurian coast. Sited atop a small hill, the lofty battlements reveal fabulous views of the Apuan Alps in northern Tuscany, famed for their Carrara marble (the scars made by the quarries are clearly visible). The castle is also home to an exhaustive archaeological museum filled with finely crafted statues, exquisite mosaics, ceramics, jewellery and even some remarkably intact glassware.

If you don't want to make the uphill slog, you can take two free lifts from either Via Indipendenza, just up from Via del Prione, or from Via XX Settembre.

ROW, ROW, ROW!

If you're in La Spezia at the beginning of August, be sure to secure a spot on the *lungomare* (seafront promenade) on the first Sunday of the month to cheer on the boats sailing by during the **Palio del Golfo** – a rowing competition between 13 *borgate* (neighbourhoods) in both La Spezia and delegations from the surrounding towns and villages. The Palio schedule is packed with events, including a nighttime parade of all *borgate* gathering to prepare for the race, a fireworks show once the Palio has been run, and a victory celebration the day immediately after.

HILLSIDE ESCAPES

The beaches of Lerici and San Terenzo are suitably inviting, but the sands can get incredibly packed during the summer months. When you need a break from the crowds, look to the hills. A network of trails runs inland, providing fabulous views over the coastline and an intriguing way of connecting towns like Lerici with Tellaro without having to step into a vehicle. And unlike the trails in Cinque Terre, you won't encounter heavy crowds while out enjoying nature. Be sure to pick up a map at a tourist office before heading out, or have a look at the trail network on lericicoast.it.

Probe the History of La Spezia's Naval Arsenal

MUSEUM

MAP: 3 P130 **D4**

Surprise! La Spezia is home to the **Museo Tecnico Navale della Spezia** *(adult/child €5/3)*, the world's oldest naval museum, reached via a narrow bridge a few blocks southwest of Parco Salvador Allende.

The interconnecting halls inside the chunky, still-functioning naval base contain all manner of maritime curiosities, including small models of sailing vessels from around the globe, otherworldly diving suits and a special area dedicated to Guglielmo Marconi's wireless invention. Upstairs, the Sala delle Polene is the most visually arresting room with two dozen figureheads that once adorned large sailing ships. The oldest, a sword- and shield-wielding Minerva, dates from 1738.

Other oddities include several WWII-era *barchini esplosivi*, torpedo-like vessels guided towards enemy ships by one or two sailors who were likely to perish during the attack.

More than Sand on Spiaggia di San Terenzo

BEACH

One of several lovely stretches of coastline in the area, **Spiaggia di San Terenzo** (MAP: 4 P135 **D1**) is a sandy beach with free sections as well as places to hire loungers and umbrellas. A long break wall, 100m offshore, ensures particularly calm waters here. As elsewhere, the crowds get thick on summer days, so go early to claim a prime spot.

Directly behind the beach, you'll see the whitewashed arches of Villa Magni, once home to British writers and poets, Percy and Mary Shelley (the latter was the author of the 1818 novel, *Frankenstein*). It is no longer open to the public but a plaque on the wall testifies to its famous former occupants.

If the beach bronzing becomes a bore, feel free to explore

PORTO VENERE & THE BAY OF POETS

For more see

Top Experiences p130
Experiences p133
Eating p139
Drinking p141
Shopping p141

Castello di San Terenzo (MAP: 5 P135 **D1**; *lericicoast.it; adult/reduced €3/2)* at its western end. Dating from the 14th century, the fortress was once part of La Spezia's powerful coastal defence system. It contains little for contemporary visitors bar fantastic views.

Enter the Chambers of Lerici Castle

CASTLE

MAP: 6 P135 **D2**

On a promontory high above the shoreline, **Castello di Lerici** *(lericicoast.it; adult/reduced €6/3)* has played a pivotal role in protecting the city since the Middle Ages. Rebuilt various times over the years, the citadel housed a paleontological museum between 1998 and 2015. Among its various stone-walled chambers, you'll find a vaulted hall, a medieval chapel and ancient kitchens. There are also fabulous views from its lofty terraces. You can download a self-guided itinerary from the website.

The easiest way to reach the castle is by taking the lift, which is hidden inside a tunnel leading off the Lerici waterfront (Via Giuseppe Mazzini). You can also follow the stairs heading up to the castle from near Piazza Garibaldi.

Castello di Lerici
SIMONA SIRIO/SHUTTERSTOCK ©

Scrutinise the Heart of Lerici

STREET

MAP: 7 P135 E1

Just off Piazza Garibaldi, the atmospheric pedestrian lane **Via Cavour** is sprinkled with colourful boutiques, a focacceria and wine shop, and some appealing seafood-focused restaurants. Anchoring the western end of the street, the sulphurous yellow facade of the Oratorio di San Rocco overlooks palm-tree lined Piazza Giuseppe Garibaldi. The original chapel dates from 1287 but was rededicated to San Rocco during a 16th-century plague when a bell tower was added.

Recline on a Beach for Poets

BEACH

MAP: 8 P135 E1

Around 1km north of Tellaro, the **Spiaggia di Fiascherino** is not one beach, but two pretty stretches of sandy shoreline separated by a small promontory. The beaches lie along curved bays and have free sections, as well as places that rent deck chairs and umbrellas. You can also hire kayaks to explore tree-lined coves nearby. Fiascherino was a favourite of DH Lawrence and snippets of his descriptive prose adorn the entrance stairway. It's easy to reach Fiascherino by bus from either Tellaro or Lerici, with a service every 30 to 60 minutes.

Slip Away to the Ruins of Portesone

RUINS

MAP: 9 P135 F2

Sequestered just off the tourist trail above Tellaro stand the ruins of **Portesone**, a former rural village that was abandoned in the 1600s, allegedly owing to a plague epidemic. Mystery hangs thickly over the falling-down stone buildings, slowly being reclaimed by the forest, with olive trees, figs and poppies growing wild in the roofless interiors.

Portesone is about a 15-minute uphill climb from Tellaro. Take trail 431 up from the main road (Via Fiascherino/SP26), located just north of the big church Stella Maris. Once you reach Portesone,

BYRON IN THE BAY

George Gordon Byron was an athlete as well as a poet. Afflicted by club foot from birth, he took up open-water swimming as a way of embracing nature and keeping in shape. Like most things Byron did, he practised it excessively and, in 1810, he became the first person to swim the 4½km between Europe and Asia across the Dardanelles. In 1822 he went one further, electing to swim 7km across the Gulf of La Spezia from Porto Venere to San Terenzo to meet up with his friends the Shelleys. Suitably impressed, the Italians renamed the bay in his honour.

Chiesa di San Giorgio, Tellaro
ALBERTO MASNOVO/SHUTTERSTOCK ©

it's possible to continue north to Barbazzano – another abandoned village – on trail 433.

Sample Tranquil Tellaro VILLAGE

MAP: 10 P135 F2

Backed by lush hillsides covered in olive trees and oaks, the faded pink and orange houses of Tellaro overlook several small bays on an effortlessly beautiful stretch of the Italian Riviera coastline, 2.5km southeast of Lerici.

Just a few narrow lanes wind through the tightly compact village, past hidden squares and surprise overlooks before reaching the rocky shore where the 16th-century **Chiesa di San Giorgio** is perched atop a spur.

Sit on the waterside square near the church and imagine an octopus ringing the bells – which, according to legend, it did to warn the villagers of a Saracen attack. An octopus festival on the second Sunday in August re-evokes the myth. There's a decent bar, La Marina (p141) , for drinks and focaccia, from where you can admire the church and the Byron-esque swimmers in the harbour.

Tellaro merits a mellow afternoon visit with an extra 90 minutes to walk over on the **Sentiero delle Parole** (Path of Words) from Lerici, following trail numbers 533 and 531. It's also possible to walk along the road (SP26).

Best Places for...

€ Budget €€ Midrange €€€ Top End

Eating

Traditional Restaurants

Osteria all'Inferno dal 1905 €€

Map p130 11 C3

This subterranean La Spezia *osteria* has been around since 1905, luring five generations of fans to its hearty plates of codfish stew, fried anchovies, wild boar with polenta and other satisfying Ligurian bites. *12.15-2.30pm & 7.30-10pm Mon-Sat*

Osteria Giobatta €€

Map p130 12 D3

This salubrious-looking joint in La Spezia's city centre is adorned with garlands hung around the windows. It lives up to its initial promise with quick, polite service and a smattering of well-rendered Ligurian classics illuminating the menu, including rabbit and sea bream. *9am-11pm*

Trattoria Bellavista €€

Map p130 13 C3

A little more à la mode than your average trattoria, La Spezia's upmarket Bella-vista proudly advertises grilled octopus, duck breast with berries, and Kobe beef tartare, which you can savour under an extravagant light fitting shaped like a tree. *noon-3pm & 7.30-11.30pm Tue-Sat*

Mediterranean Fish

Dai Pescatori €

Map p130 14 E4

Down on La Spezia's waterfront, this self-service cafeteria is a local institution and revered for its heavily-loaded plates of octopus salad, steamed mussels and fish cooked to order. Join the queue to request a table. *noon-3pm & 7-10pm Tue-Sun*

Ristorante Glam €€

Map p135 15 E2

Very Italian and suitably glam, fish dominates the proceedings at this Lerici favourite – even the *cacio e pepe* comes in a lobster sauce! Other inspirations include mussels *ragù,* tuna tacos and codfish 'meatballs'. *12.30-2.30pm & 7.30-11pm Fri-Sun & Tue, 7.30-11pm Wed & Thu*

Vicolo Intherno €€

Map p130 16 C3

Take a seat around chunky wooden tables beneath the beamed ceiling at this buzzing Slow Food–affiliated restaurant in La Spezia where *torte di verdure* (Ligurian vegetable pie), stockfish and roast beef twin with the best local vintages. *noon-3pm & 7pm-10pm Tue-Sat*

Essentiae €€

Map p135 see 10 F2

A relatively new addition to the streets of old Tellaro, Essentiae occupies a cosy slot next to the harbour and – no surprise – celebrates the fruits of the sea, headed up by an intriguing mix of steamed cod, black truffles and hazelnuts. *9am-11.45pm Wed-Mon*

Risorante Franceschini €€€
Map p135 17 D1
Exquisite presentation of fresh seafood by a young, dynamic chef gives diners ample reason to linger in San Terenzo when the beach gets too hot. For the ultimate treat, try Franceschini's eight-course tasting menu. *noon-3pm & 7-11.30pm*

Street Food

Anciua €
Map p135 18 D2
Ligurian street food made with love in a Porto Venere alley, Anciua is the ideal place to grab a *panini* stuffed with anchovies or cod and olive paste, or pick up a whole spinach pie (aka *torta*) for a picnic. *11am-7pm*

L'Oasi Focacceria €
Map p135 19 B2
Porto Venere lends itself to snacking on the harbour and L'Oasi offers far more than its name suggests (although the focaccia is outstanding). Also up for grabs are vegetable pies, meats, cheeses and fruits. *7.30am-7pm*

Off The Tourist Trail Cafes

Bar-Gelateria Dora €
Map p135 20 D3
This 'walk up and stand at the counter' bar in Porto Venere is an ideal spot for coffee and pastries before you head off on the AV5T. It's right on the harbour, with sea air wafting through the door. *8am-2am Tue-Sun*

Caffè Cavour €
Map p130 21 C3
For early-morning *colazione* (breakfast) cravings in La Spezia, join the Spezzini in this busy, tourist-free zone next to the market. Should the ambience be to your liking, feel free to come back later for an aperitif. *6am-10pm Mon-Sat*

Perfect Pizza

La Pia Centenaria €
Map p130 22 D3
Founded in 1887, La Pia is a much-loved La Spezia institution. Piping hot slices of *farinata* (chickpea flour flat bread) is the big draw, supported by perfectly cooked slabs of pizza, satisfying focaccia and quiche-like vegetable *torta*. *11am-10pm Mon-Sat*

Pizzeria Masaniello €€
Map p130 23 C1
Catch some rays in the glassed-in awning of Masaniello on La Spezia's Via Fiume, tucking into chewy, thick-crusted pizza that looks like it's just been teleported over from Naples. All you need to know! *11am-11pm*

Ice Cream

Gelateria La Dolce Vita €
Map p130 24 D3
For urgent ice cream fixes in La Spezia head directly to 'The Sweet Life' under the porticoes opposite the public gardens, where strolling and people-watching go down well with a large cone. *11am-11.30pm*

Gelateria Arcobaleno Lerici €
Map p130 see 7 E1
Let the over-sized ice-cream cone in Lerici's Piazza Giuseppe Garibaldi guide you to this narrow little gelato outlet, home to some two dozen ravishing flavours that'll enhance your enjoyment of the promenade. *noon-12.30am*

Drinking

Bars, Cafes & Drinking Dens

Odioilvino

Map p130 25 D3

A dark, bohemian, artfully dishevelled wine bar on a pretty street in La Spezia's pedestrian centre, Odioilvino is a fine place to relax with locals over Ligurian wine and local craft beer. *11.30am-3pm & 5.30-11pm Mon-Sat*

Resilience Cafe

Map p130 26 E3

A bar-cafe that could have been plucked from Genoa or even Paris' Latin Quarter, the Resilience in La Spezia combines cool elegance with enough scrumptious snacks to take the edge off your pre-dinner appetite. *6pm-midnight Mon-Thu, to 1am Fri & Sat*

La Taverna del Metallo

Map p130 27 C2

A heart-warming combination of heavy metal music and faux medieval decor draws young revellers to this quirky drinking den just off La Spezia's Via del Prione. *8pm-2am*

Bar la Marina

Map p135 see 10 F2

Situated at the end of the road in the Golfo dei Poeti, this unpretentious bar with a terrace overlooking Tellaro's diminutive marina allows you to contemplate the terracotta-red San Giorgio church while downing Peroni, Aperol *spritz* or coffee. *10am-10pm*

La Spezia Brewing Company

Map p130 28 A1

Founded by two Swedes in 2016, La Spezia Brewing Company concocts some of the finest beers on the Italian Riviera. Tipples range from a light Berliner (a Weisse beer) to a 7.8% Ciocancia stout. *4-8pm Wed-Sat*

Shopping

Fragrance

Gocce di Byron

Map p135 29 D3

With a grotto and bay named in his honour, why not a perfumery? Awash with pleasant aromas, the potently scented 'Drops of Byron' in Porto Venere sells fragrances named after enchanting places around the region. *10am-1pm & 3-7pm*

Food & Drink

Piazza del Mercato

Map p130 30 C2

Held in a covered square in the centre of La Spezia, this tourist-free market is a lively place to browse for fresh fruits, vegetables, cheeses, olives and other potential picnic items. *6am-2pm Mon-Sat*

Drogheria Stoppani & Peer

Map p130 31 D3

Fifth-generation La Spezia grocery store in business since 1855 with a busy, well-curated interior crammed with spices, chocolate, preserves, sauces, tea and coffee. It makes for an intriguing browse even if you're not buying. *9am-12.30pm & 4-7.30pm Tue-Sat, 4-7.30pm Mon*

Books

Cartolibreria Castagnasso

Map p130 32 B2

Historic book and stationery shop in La Spezia, dating from 1877 that brims with writing materials, school supplies, novels, classics and a particularly well-stocked selection of children's books. *9am-12.45pm & 3.45-7.45pm Mon-Sat*

Genoa & Cinque Terre Toolkit

Genoa (p33)

SERGII FIGURNYI/SHUTTERSTOCK ©

Family Travel

A family trip to the Riviera is justifiable for the gelato alone. Throw in pizza, pasta, Europe's second-largest aquarium and some of Italy's best beaches, and you might just have enough to tear your bored teenager away from their precious phone.

Baby Requirements

Baby requirements are easily met (except on Sundays when most shops are closed). Pharmacies and supermarkets sell baby formula, nappies (diapers), ready-made baby food and sterilising solutions. Fresh cow's milk is sold in cartons in supermarkets and in bars with a 'Latteria' sign.

BEACH CLUBS

Seemingly made with families in mind, Liguria's *stabilimenti balneari* (beach clubs) offer a stress-free day at the beach for a small fee (€15–50), with life-guards, changing cabins, showers, restaurants, plus parasols and sun-loungers thrown in.

Eating Out With Kids

Kids are welcome pretty much everywhere, especially in casual, family-run trattorias. These places are usually refreshingly informal with friendly, indulgent wait staff and menus of simple pasta dishes and grilled meats. Pizzerias are another option and once you've got to grips with the Italian approach to toppings (often just one or two ingredients plus tomato and mozzarella) you'll be a fan for life.

Italia Kids

Italia Kids *(italiakids.com)* is a family travel and lifestyle guide to Italy, packed with practical tips and accommodation listings.

Ciao Bambino

Ciao Bambino *(ciao bambino.com)* offers tours, activities, recommendations and planning advice, put together by family-travel experts.

Accommodation

In cities and towns, family and four-person rooms can be hard to find and should be booked in advance. Alternatively, plenty of hotels and boutique B&Bs offer family-friendly, self-catering apartments.

Accommodation

A mix of urban and rural accommodation is on offer in Liguria, ranging from palatial villas in Portofino to economical, next-to-the-station hostels in Genoa.

Where to Stay if You Love...

The Atmosphere of Genoa's Historic 'Hood

The *caruggi* (p44) It's crowded and a little cramped but everything is on your doorstep, from trattorias to churches, and there's a palpable sense of history.

We Love to Stay in...

Corniglia (p99)

If you want a taste of Cinque Terre without an endless stream of tourists surging past your door, book a room in Corniglia, the smallest of the coastal quintet that transforms into a quieter, more authentic realm after 5pm. The village excels in tastefully furnished apartments, many with sea views.

Posh Digs, No Expense Spared

Portofino (p53)
Experience a quieter version of Portofino after the crowds go home and only those wealthy enough to afford a hotel room stalk the famous Piazzetta.

Instant Beach Access

Levanto (p64) Staying over means you can get up early in this buzzing Italian beach town and reserve your spot on the sand or sun-lounger.

A Room With a View

Manarola (p109) A vertical village of tall traditional houses facing the sea, most of Manarola's apartments, B&Bs and boutique hotels offer spectacular views.

An Elegant Resort

Santa Margherita Ligure (p61)
A notch down from Portofino price-wise but without a noticeable drop in quality, plus close proximity to a train station.

HOW MUCH FOR A NIGHT IN...

Hostel dorm bed
€36

Cinque Terre apartment
€110

Double room in palatial hotel in Genoa
€195

Food, Drink & Nightlife

Allergies and Intolerances

Italy has a reasonably good handle on the nuances of food allergies, with some intolerances catered for better than others. If you have ultra-specific eating requirements, book accommodation with kitchen facilities and wise up on basic Italian phrases to use in restaurants and shops.

Wheat Grano
Milk/cream Latte/Crema
Eggs Uova
Shellfish Crostacei
Coeliac Celiaco

?
HOW TO ASK...
Is this gluten-free?
E' senza glutine?
Does this contain nuts?
Questo contiene noci?
Is there a vegan option?
C'è un'opzione vegana?

RESERVATIONS

Italy has no shortage of eating options, and reserving a table on the day of your meal is usually fine. Top-end restaurants may need to be booked a month or more in advance, while popular eateries in tourist areas should be booked at least a few days ahead in peak season.

Takeout Focaccia

Liguria's ultimate take-out food is focaccia: flat oven-baked bread punctuated with small finger-sized holes and sold in local bakeries, cafes and specialist focaccerias. It's usually offered *al taglio* (by the slice) and priced by weight. Locals often enjoy it with a cappuccino for breakfast.

Pay the Bill

Most cafes and bars are staffed with servers who'll attend to you at your table, bringing you the bill on request. Ask for *'il conto'* or make the internationally understood finger-thumb rubbing sign.

In small local bars, it's more common to order and enjoy your drink at the bar. Pay the barperson directly afterwards.

Credit cards are widely accepted in cafes and restaurants, even if you're just buying a cup of coffee.

Splitting the bill isn't common practice among Italians. However, you can request to do so by saying: *'Potete farci conti separati?'*

PRICE RANGES

The following average price ranges refer to a meal of two courses and a glass of house wine.

€ less than €25
€€ €25-45
€€€ more than €45

OPENING HOURS

Restaurants
noon–3pm & 7.30pm–11pm (later in summer)

Bars & cafes
7.30am–8pm, sometimes to 1am or 2am

Clubs
10pm–4am or 5am

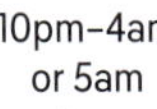

Going Out

Genoa is a big city with a decent late-night scene. Cinque Terre and Portofino go to bed much earlier.

Aperitifs Pre-dinner drinks are a tradition throughout the region with Aperol *spritz* being the default cocktail. Prime spots for a pleasant water view include Genoa's Porto Antico (p34), Boccadasse (p47), Portofino's Piazzetta (p60), and anywhere in Cinque Terre.

Clubs Most of Genoa's late-night action is located outside the historic core with several big-name clubs and discos centred on the Corso Italia (p47).

Genoa's Drinking Hubs

Never underestimate the lure of the *caruggi* (narrow streets) for nighttime fun. You'll find a number of trendy drinking spots, including Les Rouges and Malkovich (p50), intermingled with old-time favourites throughout the historic quarter, particularly in the streets just northwest of Piazza de Ferrari (p43). Piazza delle Erbe (p51) pulls the city's young for cheap and cheerful *aperitivi* (predinner drinks) and often remains rowdy well into the night.

HOW MUCH FOR A...

cappuccino
€1.50-2

brioche (croissant)
€2-3

pizza margherita
€8-13

primi (first course)
€8-15

secondi (second course)
€15-25

aperitif
€8-10

beer
€6

FROM LEFT: TASSANEET/SHUTTERSTOCK ©, PROXIMA STUDIO/SHUTTERSTOCK ©

LGBTIQ+ Travellers

Italy is considered one of the world's most tolerant countries when it comes to sexual orientation. Same-sex civil unions have been legal since 2016.

The Scene

Genoa As a large city, Genoa has several gay clubs and bars although the scene isn't as big as Rome or Milan. **Virgo Disco Club** (facebook.com/virgo.discoclub) is a venue a little to the west of the Porto Antico.

Cinque Terre doesn't really have a gay culture per se but the general atmosphere is accepting and congenial. Public shows of affection between same-sex couples don't turn heads and anyone can pledge undying love on the romantic Via dell'Amore.

LAW EVOLUTION

- Homosexuality decriminalised in 1890.
- Transgender people allowed to change legal gender since 1982.
- Same-sex civil unions – but not same-sex marriage – allowed since 2016. Same-sex couples still don't have the same adoption and IVF access rights as married couples.

OUR PICKS

Our Pick

Gaily Tour (*gailytour.com*) is an Italian-based tour operator that organises LGBTIQ+ friendly excursions to some of Europe's popular tourist spots. It offers two Cinque Terre tours (half- and full-day) that start in La Spezia and incorporate four of the five villages (all except Corniglia). Tour guides impart copious information and include some local LGBTIQ+ history in the discussion.

LIGURIA PRIDE

The region's main annual Pride event, Liguria Pride, takes place in Genoa in the first week in June spearheaded by a parade that culminates in Piazza de Ferrari.

Resources

- **www.prideonline.it** Scan this code for culture, politics, travel and health with an LGBTIQ+ focus.

Health & Safe Travel

Italy has a public health system (Servizio Sanitario Nazionale, SSN) that is legally bound to provide emergency care to everyone.

Pharmacies

Pharmacies, marked by a green cross, generally keep shop hours, typically opening from 8.30am to 7.30pm Monday to Friday and on Saturday mornings. Outside these hours, they open on a rotational basis. When closed, a pharmacy is legally required to post a list of places open in the vicinity.

Pharmacists can advise on medical matters and sell over-the-counter medications for minor illnesses. They can also point you in the right direction if you need more specialised help.

DRINKING WATER

Tap water in Genoa and Cinque Terre is safe to drink unless a tap is marked *'acqua non potabile'* (water not suitable for drinking). Even the smallest villages in Liguria have a public tap or fountain in the main piazza dispensing fresh drinking water.

Calling an Ambulance

If you need an ambulance anywhere in Italy, call 118.

Pickpocketing

Genoa and Cinque Terre are generally safe places to travel in. Note, however, that petty theft can be a problem – pickpockets and thieves are active in tourist areas and on crowded public transport. In case of theft or loss, always report the incident to the police within 24 hours and ask for a statement.

EMERGENCY TREATMENT

For emergency treatment, head to the *pronto soccorso* (casualty department) of an *ospedale* (public hospital), where you can also get emergency dental treatment.

QUICK INFO

EU nationals are entitled to reduced-cost, and sometimes free, medical care with a **European Health Insurance Card** (EHIC), available from your home health authority. Non-EU citizens, including UK citizens, should take out medical insurance.

Responsible Travel

Follow these tips to leave a lighter footprint, support local businesses and have a positive impact on communities.

Local Food

Local food is easy to procure in Ligurian restaurants. Just walk into any trattoria or *osteria* (casual eatery) and order anything made with pesto, anchovies, lemons, olive oil, rabbit or a dozen different cheeses, from Prescinseua to Caciotta di Brugnata. Local drinks are also well covered, with straw-coloured white wines like Cinque Terre DOC and the delightfully sweet dessert wine, Sciacchetrà. *Limoncino* is a lemon liqueur similar to southern Italy's *limoncello*.

Public Transport

The Riviera is arguably the best connected of all Italian regions when it comes to public transportation. Even the smallest villages have a train station and/or a reliable bus connection.

Sustainably-minded travel agency **Arbaspàa** (p115) in Manarola offers a Cinque Terre farm tour that'll teach you about olive growing, bee breeding and small-scale wine production.

Agriturismi

Live out your bucolic fantasies at one of Italy's growing number of *agriturismi* (farm stays). While all *agriturismi* are required to grow at least one of their own products, the farm stays themselves range from rustic country houses with a handful of olive trees to elegant country estates with sparkling pools to fully functioning farms where guests can pitch in.

Resources

• **agriturismo.it** Farm stays • **slowfood.com** Slow Food • **parconazionale5terre.it** Parco Nazionale delle Cinque Terre • **parks.it/parco.portofino** Parco Naturale Regionale di Portofino • **parks.it/parco.porto.venere** Parco Naturale Regionale di Porto Venere

FROM LEFT: ALESSIO ORRU/SHUTTERSTOCK ©, CHRISTIAN MUELLER/SHUTTERSTOCK ©, ALESSIO ORRU/SHUTTERSTOCK ©

NATIONAL & REGIONAL PARKS

Liguria is protected with one national park, Cinque Terre (designated in 1999) and two regional nature parks, Porto Venere (including the village and the islands of Palmaria, Tino and Tinetto) and the Portofino peninsula.

Slow Food & Slow Fish

Genoa is the host of the Slow Food movement's annual pescatarian shindig, Slow Fish, held in Porto Antico over four days in June every odd-numbered year.

The city has over a dozen of its restaurants featured in the annually updated Slow Food guide to Italian osterie, including Rosmarino (p48), Sà Pesta (p49) and Trattoria delle Grazie (p48).

WORK ON AN ORGANIC FARM

For a small annual membership fee, World Wide Opportunities on Organic Farms *(wwoof.it)* provides a list of farms in Italy looking for volunteer workers.

Climate Change & Travel

It's impossible to ignore the impact we have when travelling; Lonely Planet urges all travellers to engage with their travel carbon footprint, which will mainly come from air travel. While there often isn't an alternative, travellers can look to minimise the number of flights they take, opt for newer aircrafts and use cleaner ground transport, such as trains. One proposed solution – purchasing carbon offsets – unfortunately does not cancel out the impact of individual flights. While most destinations will depend on air travel for the foreseeable future, for now, pursuing ground-based travel where possible is the best course of action.

The **UN Carbon Offset Calculator** shows how flying impacts a household's emissions

The **ICAO's carbon emissions calculator** allows visitors to analyse the CO_2 generated by point-to-point journeys

Accessible Travel

Public Lifts & Escalators

The steep hills and vertical terrain of much of Liguria can cause problems for accessibility. Fortunately many places have public lifts (elevators) to bypass the copious flights of stairs.

Places with lifts include Genoa (10 in total), Riomaggiore, Lerici and La Spezia. Public lifts generally cost €2 to use.

Train Stations

Genoa's Piazza Principe station has special Sala Blu offices offering free help to everyone from wheelchair users to the visually impaired to pregnant women. Other stations with PRM assistance include Santa Margherita Ligure-Portofino, Rapallo, Levanto and Monterosso. Reserve ahead on +39 02 32 32 32 (outside Italy) or 800 90 60 60 (inside Italy).

BUSES & TAXIS

Many urban buses are wheelchair-accessible; however, some of the stops may not be – ask before you board. Some taxis are equipped to carry passengers in wheelchairs; ask for a taxi for a *sedia a rotelle* (wheelchair).

Museum Reductions

Many museums and galleries offer free admission to people with a disability (and/or appropriate ID) plus a companion.

Genoa's Musei di Strada Nuova (p38) gives a €2 reduction if you have a disability card, plus free entry for chaperones.

Genoa's **Galata Museo del Mare** (p46) has tactile maps for the visually impaired, amplification devices for the hearing impaired, blue badge parking, indoor electric scooters and mega-wide ramped walkways between floors that are easy to negotiate. Companion dogs are welcome for people with disabilities. On top of all this, the museum is exceedingly well put together both visually and educationally. You could easily spend half a day here.

PARKING PERMITS

If you are driving, EU disabled parking permits are recognised in Italy, giving you the same parking rights as local drivers with disabilities.

Resources

- **villageforall.net/en** Village for All performs on-site audits of tourist facilities in Italy.

Nuts & Bolts

Opening Hours

Summer hours (April to September)

Banks
8.30am–1.30pm and 2.45pm–4.30pm Monday to Friday

Bars & cafes
7.30am–8pm, sometimes to 1am or 2am

Clubs
10pm–4am or 5am

Restaurants
noon–3pm and 7.30pm–11pm)

Shops
9am–1pm and 3.30pm–7.30pm (or 4pm to 8pm) Monday to Saturday. In main cities some shops stay open at lunchtime and on Sunday mornings. Some shops close Monday mornings.

QUICK INFO

Time zone
Central European Time Zone (GMT/ UTC plus one hour)

City calling code
010

Emergency number
112

Population (Genoa)
580,000

Toilets

Besides in museums, galleries, department stores and train stations, there are few public toilets in Italy. If you're caught short, the best thing to do is to nip into a cafe or bar. The polite thing to do is to order something at the bar. You usually have to pay to use public toilets.

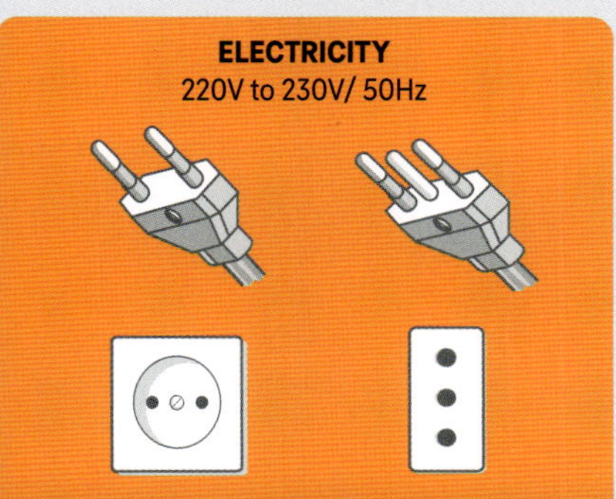

Public Holidays

National public holidays include the following.

Capodanno
New Year's Day, 1 January

Epifania
Epiphany, 6 January

Pasquetta
Easter Monday, March/April

Giorno della Liberazione
Liberation Day, 25 April

Festa del Lavoro
Labour Day, 1 May

Festa della Repubblica
Republic Day, 2 June

Ferragosto
Feast of the Assumption, 15 August

Festa di Ognissanti
All Saints' Day, 1 November

Festa dell'Immacolata Concezione
Feast of the Immaculate Conception, 8 December

Natale
Christmas Day, 25 December

Festa di Santo Stefano
Boxing Day, 26 December

Aperto
Open
Chiuso
Closed

Language

Italian Basics

Hello.
Buongiorno.
bwon·jor·no

Goodbye.
Arrivederci.
a·ree·ve·der·che

Yes.
Sì. *see*

No.
No. *no*

Please.
Per favore.
per fa·vo·re

Thank you.
Grazie. *gra·tsye*

Excuse me.
Mi scusi. (pol)
mee skoo·zee
Scusami. (inf)
skoo·za·me

You're welcome.
Prego. *pre·go*

Fast Phrases

Do you speak English?
Parla inglese? (pol) *par·la een·gle·z*
Parli inglese? (inf) *par·lee inglese?*

I don't understand. **Non capisco.** *non ka·pee·sko*

I'd like... **Vorrei.** *vo·ray*
a beer. **una birra.** *oona bee·ra*
a coffee. **un caffè.** *oon ka·fe*
a white wine. **un vino bianco.** *oon vee·no byan·ko*
a red wine. **un vino rosso.** *oon vee·no ro·so*

Please bring the bill.
Mi porta il conto, per favore. *mee por·ta eel kon·to per fa·vo·re*

How much is this?
Quanto costa questo? *kwan·to kos·ta kwe·sto*

Where is the toilet?
Dov'è il bagno? *do·ve eel ba·nyo*

Could you please speak more slowly?
Può parlare più lentamente, per favore? (pol)
pwo par·la·re pyoo len·ta·men·te per fa·vo·re
Puoi parlare più lentamente, per favore? (inf)
pwoy par·la·re pyoo len·ta·men·te per fa·vo·re

Where's an ATM?
Dov'è un Bancomat? *do·ve oon ban·ko·mat*

Slowly, please!
Più lentamente, per favore! *pyoo len·ta·men·te per fa·vo·re*

Numbers

uno
oo·no

due
doo·e

tre
tre

quattro
kwa·tro

cinque
cheen·kwe

Good to Know

In Italian, you generally emphasise the second-last syllable in a word. However, when a written word has an accent marked on a vowel, the stress is on that syllable.

The characteristic sing-song quality of an Italian sentence is created by pronouncing the syllables evenly and rhythmically, then swinging down on the last word.

Italian has a formal and informal word for 'you' (lei *lay* and tu *too* respectively); the verbs have a different ending for each person.

ITALIAN IN ITALY

Italians are very proud of their language's rich history and influence – rightly so, since it claims the closest relationship with the language spoken by the Romans. For example, Italy is one of the few countries in Europe where dubbing of foreign-language movies is preferred to subtitling.

Signs

Aperto Open
Chiuso Closed
Spingere Push
Tirare Pull
Uscita Exit
Entrata Entry
Donne Women
Uomini Men
Bagno (WC) Toilets
Stazione Train station
Aeroporto Airport
Non fumatore Non-smoking

Listen for

Il suo passaporto per favore. *eel soo·o pa·sa·por·to per fa·vo·re.* **Your passport please.**

Il suo visto, per favore. *eel soo·o vees·to per fa·vo·re* **Your visa, please.**

10 PHRASES TO SOUND LIKE A LOCAL

What's up? **Cosa c'é?** *ko·za che*
All OK? **Tutto a posto?** *too·ta pos·to*
It's OK. **Va bene.** *va be·ne*
Great! **Fantastico!** *fan·tas·tee·ko*
That's true. **È vero.** *e ve·ro*
Sure. **Certo.** *cher·to*
No way! **Per niente!** *per nyen·te*
You're kidding! **Scherzi!** *sker·tsee*
If only! **Magari!** *ma·ga·ree*
Really? **Davvero?** *da·ve·ro*

6	7	8	9	10
sei	**sette**	**otto**	**nove**	**dieci**
say	*se·te*	*o·to*	*no·ve*	*dye·chee*

Index

Sights p000 Map pages p000

See also separate subindexes for:
Eating p158
Drinking p159
Shopping p159

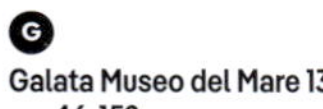

G

H

I

K

L

M

N

O

P

Eating

Drinking

Shopping

Send Us Your Feedback

We love to hear from travellers – your comments help make our books better. We read every word, and we guarantee that your feedback goes straight to the authors. Visit lonelyplanet.com/contact to submit your updates and suggestions.

Note: We may edit, reproduce and incorporate your comments in Lonely Planet products such as guidebooks, websites and digital products, so let us know if you are happy to have your name acknowledged. For a copy of our privacy policy visit lonelyplanet.com/legal.

Acknowledgements

Front-cover photograph: Beach, Sestri Levante. Chris Curry/Unsplash ©

Back-cover photograph: Beach, Abbazia di San Fruttuoso. Francesco Bonino/Shutterstock ©

THIS BOOK

Destination Editor
Daniel Bolger

Cartographer
Rachel Imeson

Production Editor
Claire Rourke

Assisting Editors
Anita Isalska, Fionnuala Twomey

Book Designer
Compton Sheldon

Cover Researcher
Front cover: Lauren Egan
Back cover: Compton Sheldon

Thanks to
Sofie Andersen, Imogen Bannister, Fergal Condon, Melanie Dankel, Ania Lenihan

Published by Lonely Planet Global Limited
CRN 554153
2nd edition – Apr 2025
ISBN 978 1 78868 412 5

10 9 8 7 6 5 4 3 2 1
Printed in China